21
DAYS TO

Find
Success
and
Inner Peace

Also in the 21 Days series

21
DAYS TO

Find
Success
and
Inner Peace

Live with Gratitude, Connect to Spirit,
and Find Purpose, Strength, and Joy

DR. WAYNE W. DYER

HAY HOUSE

Carlsbad, California • New York City
London • Sydney • New Delhi

Published in the United Kingdom by:
Hay House UK Ltd, The Sixth Floor, Watson House,
54 Baker Street, London W1U 7BU
Tel: +44 (0)20 3927 7290; www.hayhouse.co.uk

Published in the United States of America by:
Hay House Inc., PO Box 5100, Carlsbad, CA 92018-5100
Tel: (1) 760 431 7695 or (800) 654 5126; www.hayhouse.com

Published in Australia by:
Hay House Australia Pty Ltd, 18/36 Ralph St, Alexandria NSW 2015
Tel: (61) 2 9669 4299; www.hayhouse.com.au

Published in India by:
Hay House Publishers India, Muskaan Complex,
Plot No.3, B-2, Vasant Kunj, New Delhi 110 070
Tel: (91) 11 4176 1620; www.hayhouse.co.in

Text © Dr. Wayne W. Dyer, 2011, 2022

21 Days to Find Success and Inner Peace draws from Dr. Wayne W. Dyer's bestselling *10 Secrets for Success and Inner Peace* (Hay House, 2001) and *Inspiration* (Hay House, 2006).

The moral rights of the author have been asserted.

The information given in this book should not be treated as a substitute for professional medical advice; always consult a medical practitioner. Any use of information in this book is at the reader's discretion and risk. Neither the author nor the publisher can be held responsible for any loss, claim or damage arising out of the use, or misuse, of the suggestions made, the failure to take medical advice or for any material on third-party websites.

A catalogue record for this book is available from the British Library.

Tradepaper ISBN: 978-1-4019-7120-5
E-book ISBN: 978-1-78817-894-5
Audiobook ISBN: 978-1-78817-851-8

Interior illustrations: Shutterstock

Printed in the United States of America

10 9 8 7 6 5 4 3 2 1

Contents

Publisher's Note

Research has shown that establishing a habit requires 21 days' practice. That's why Hay House has decided to adapt the work of some of its most prestigious authors into these short, 21-day courses, designed specifically to develop new mastery of subjects such as success and inner peace.

Other titles that will help you to explore further the concepts featured in this 21-day program are listed at the beginning of this book.

21 Days to Find Success and Inner Peace draws from Wayne W. Dyer's best-selling *10 Secrets for Success and Inner Peace* (Hay House, 2001) and *Inspiration* (Hay House, 2006).

Introduction

There's never a day that goes by that I don't think about God. More than thinking, I experience the presence of God in most of my waking moments. It's a feeling of contentment and satisfaction that's beyond anything that I might convey in a book. I've come to know the peace of Spirit in my life, and because of this knowing, all of my concerns, problems, accomplishments, and accumulations diminish in importance. In this short book, I will elaborate on principles to success and inner peace, which, if mastered and practiced on a daily basis, will also guide you to this same sense of tranquility.

These principles are valuable for anyone who has decided to consciously be on their life path. Each of us makes that choice depending on our individual time clock. For some, it's early in young adulthood; and for others, it happens in the middle or mature years. The principles apply whether you're just beginning your life path, are nearing the end of it, or are on the path in any way.

Most books of this sort stress the importance of hard work, dedication, financial planning, relationship strategies, choosing the right career, listening to one's elders, being respectful of the rules, setting realistic goals, living a healthy lifestyle, and being in a state of gratitude. This is good advice and certainly benefits those who choose to listen to and apply this wisdom. It is my experience, however, both as a lifelong teacher and a father of eight children, that this kind of advice by itself leads one to wondering, *Is that all there is?*

So, I have no advice on goal setting, putting your nose to the grindstone, planning your financial future, listening to older folks, respecting your culture, and so on. In fact, I've almost always listened to my own impulses, paying the price for taking the road "least traveled" and resisting enculturation, so it would be somewhat hypocritical of me to now tell you to do what I say and follow my rules. Instead, what I offer you are principles that allow your spirit to guide you.

In my experience working with a variety of people over several decades, far too many individuals choose to be anonymous members of the pack, therefore suffering from the inner remorse that makes them feel like failures, filled with conflict and resentment and wondering what the meaning of life is.

So, I've written this book in the hopes that it will help you avoid those feelings of inadequacy and help you feel the peace of God that truly defines success. Read these principles with an open heart. Apply the ones that resonate with you, and discard those that don't.

When you feel peaceful and successful, you want to extend and export that peace and love. The violence, hatred, prejudice, and judgment in our world suggest that we have miles to go to reach a world of inner and outer peace.

I send you love and all green lights.

DAY 1

Be Open to Everything

One of the fundamental keys to success and inner peace is allowing yourself to be open to the infinite array of possibilities in your life. This is our topic for today.

Having a mind that is open to everything sounds easy until you think about how much conditioning has taken place in your life, and how many of your current thoughts were influenced by geography, the religious beliefs of your ancestors, the color of your skin, the political orientation of your parents, your size, your gender, the schools that were selected for you, and the vocation of your great-grandparents, to list only some possibilities.

You showed up here as a tiny infant capable of an infinite number of potentialities. Many of your choices remain unexplored because of a hopefully well-intentioned conditioning program designed to make you fit the culture of your caretakers. You probably had next to no opportunity to disagree with the cultural and societal arrangements made for your life.

There may have been some adults who encouraged you to have an open mind, but if you're honest with yourself, you know that your philosophy of life, your religious beliefs, your manner of dress, and your language are a function of what your society (and its heritage) determined was right for you. If you made any fuss about going against this preordained conditioning, you probably heard even stronger voices insisting that you get back in line and do things the way they have "always been done." Fitting in superseded having a mind that was open to new ideas.

Whatever the reasons our ancestors may have had for not having open minds, it's true that they inhabited a much less populated world than we do. In today's overpopulated world, we simply cannot continue to live with those old styles of closed-mindedness.

Everything means just what it says. No exceptions. When someone suggests something to you that conflicts with your conditioning, rather than responding with, "That's ridiculous; we all know that's impossible," say, "I've never considered that before. I'll think about it." Open yourself up to the spiritual ideas of all people, and listen with an open mind to crazy schemes and ideas that at first seem to be outrageous. If someone suggests that crystals can cure hemorrhoids, that natural herbs can lower cholesterol, that people will eventually be able to breathe underwater, or that levitation is possible—listen, and be curious.

I urge you to open your mind to *all* possibilities, to resist any efforts to be pigeonholed, and to refuse to allow pessimism into your consciousness. Having a mind that is open to everything seems to me to be one of the most basic principles that you can adopt to contribute to individual and world peace.

No One Knows Enough to Be a Pessimist

Find an opportunity to observe a tiny little green sprout emerging from a seed. When you do, allow yourself to feel the awe of what you're seeing. The Sufi poet Rumi observed, "Sell your cleverness and purchase bewilderment." The scene of an emerging sprout represents the beginning of life. No one on this planet has even a tiny clue as to how all this works. What is that creative spark that causes the life to sprout? What created the observer, the consciousness, the observation, and perception itself? The questions are endless.

Nowadays, scientists in the space program can move a tiny vehicle on Mars via remote control. Invisible signals take 10 minutes to travel through space and arrive to make right turns and instruct a scoop to pick up some Martian real estate to examine. We all marvel at such technological feats. But think about it for a moment. In an endless universe, Mars, our closest neighbor, is the equivalent of moving a billionth of an inch across the page you're reading! We move a little vehicle on a neighbor next door and we're so impressed with ourselves.

There are billions and billions of planets, objects, and stars in our galaxy alone, and there are uncountable billions of galaxies out there. This planet is a speck in an incomprehensibly vast universe that has no end. Think about this: If we found the end, would there be a wall at the edge of the universe? If so, who built it? Even more perplexing, what's on the other side of the wall, and how thick is it?

How can anyone be a pessimist in a world where we know so little? A heart starts beating inside a mother's womb a few weeks after conception, and it's a total mystery to everyone on our planet. In comparison to what there is to know, we are only embryos. Keep this in mind whenever you encounter those who are absolutely certain that there's only one way to do something.

Resist being a pessimist. Resist with all your might, because we hardly know anything at all in comparison with what there is to know. Can you imagine what a pessimist who lived only 200 years ago would think about the world we live in? Airplanes, electricity, automobiles, television, remote controls, the Internet, fax machines, telephones, cellular phones, and so on—and all available to us because of that spark of open-mindedness that allowed progress, growth, and creativity to flourish.

And what of the future and all of your tomorrows? Can you picture faxing yourself back to the 14th century, flying without machines, telepathically communicating, de-molecularizing yourself and rearranging yourself on another galaxy, or cloning a sheep from a photograph of a sheep? An open mind allows you to explore and create and grow. A closed mind seals off any such creative explanation. Remember that progress would be impossible if we always did things the way we always have. The ability to participate in miracles—true miracles in your life—happens when you open your mind to your limitless potential.

The Miracle Mind-set

Refuse to allow yourself to have low expectations about what you're capable of creating. As Michelangelo suggested, the greater danger is not that your hopes are too high and you fail to reach them; it's that they're too low and you do. Have within you an imaginary candle flame that burns brightly regardless of what goes before you. Let this inner flame represent for you the idea that you're capable of manifesting miracles in your life.

In every single case of a person experiencing a spontaneous healing or overcoming something that was considered to be impossible, the individual went through a complete reversal of personality. They actually rewrote their own agreement with reality. To experience Godlike spontaneous miracles, you must have a sense of yourself as Godlike. The Scriptures say, "With God all things are possible." Now tell me, what does that leave out? A mind that's open to everything means being peaceful, radiating love, practicing forgiveness, being generous, respecting all life, and most important, visualizing yourself as capable of doing anything that you can conceive of in your mind and heart. Whatever universal law that has ever been utilized to manifest a miracle anywhere, any time, and in any person is still on the books. It has never been repealed, and it never will be. You possess the same energy, the same God consciousness, to be a miracle worker—but only if you truly believe and know it within yourself.

Understand that what you think about expands ("As a man thinketh, so is he"). If your thoughts are filled with doubt and you have a closed mind, you'll of necessity act upon those closed-minded doubts, and you'll see evidence of your thinking virtually everywhere you are. On the other hand, should you decide (make no mistake about this, it is a choice) to have a mind that's open to everything, then you'll act upon that inner energy, and you'll be the creator as well as the recipient of miracles wherever you are. You will experience what Walt Whitman meant when he wrote, "To me, every cubic inch of space is a miracle."

DAY 2

Be Attached to Nothing

Once you decide to open your mind to everything, the next step is to let go of all your attachments. We are going to look at this topic today.

A good place to start is to let go of your attachments to what you've been trained to believe. Open your mind to all possibilities, because whether you believe something is possible or impossible, either way you'll be right. How can that be true? Your agreement with reality and all that's possible determines what you'll become. If you're convinced that you can't become wealthy, famous, artistic, a professional athlete, a great singer, or whatever, you will act upon that inner conviction that prevents you from manifesting what you'd really like. All that you'll get from your effort is being right. When you need to be right, you're attached to your conditioned reflex of the way things are and always have been; and you assume they will always be.

Releasing Your Attachments

Your attachments are the source of all your problems. The need to be right, to possess someone or something, to win at all costs, to be viewed by others as superior—these are all attachments. The open mind resists these attachments and consequently experiences inner peace and success.

If you think peaceful thoughts, you'll feel peaceful emotions, and that's what you'll bring to every life situation. If you're attached to being right or absolutely need something in order to be at peace or to be successful, you'll live a life of striving yet never arriving.

To release attachments, you have to make a shift in how you view yourself. If your primary identification is with your body and your possessions, your ego is the dominant force in your life. If you can tame your ego sufficiently, you'll call upon your spirit to be the guiding force in your life. As a spiritual being, you can observe your body and be a compassionate witness to your existence. Your spiritual aspect sees the folly of attachments because your spiritual self is an infinite soul. Nothing can make you happy or successful. These are inner constructs that you bring to your world, rather than what you receive from it.

However, releasing your attachment, especially to possessions, is not easy in this consumer-oriented world in which you are bombarded by advertising that continually exhorts you to buy bigger, better, more. The first step in transcending such messages is to become aware of what's going on and realize that you don't really need anything else in order to be happy. You may need to say this to yourself over and over until it sinks in: "Nothing can make me happy. Happiness is what I bring to life, not what I purchase." This awareness diminishes the annoyance of all those commercial messages, and at the same time allows you to enjoy their creativity, because you've detached from the ego messages and connected to Spirit.

What I'm suggesting is that you can be free from the push to convince yourself that you need more, while still being able to enjoy the material aspects of the world. In other words, you know that you don't need more, and at the same time, you're free to live happily and enjoy the world the way it is. I want this distinction to be clear because it's fun enjoying a new automobile, well-made clothes, dinner in a nice restaurant, an expensive piece of jewelry, or anything else (including this book). What you want to avoid is the inner belief that somehow your true essence is lacking if you don't get more possessions. You must also guard against allowing this "stuff" to define your worthiness, which is what advertisers frequently attempt to convey.

When I allowed my awareness to purchase only what I desired, I found myself less and less attached to stuff. You see, the more I have, the more it becomes almost burdensome to store it, insure it, dust it, decide if it's tax deductible, and ultimately dispose of it. These days I'm almost amused by the advertising I'm subjected to, and when it appears, I press my "spiritual mute button" and feel even happier that I'm immune to the message that certain brands can add status to my life.

Trust Your Inner Vision

It's possible to have a burning desire yet not have attachments. You can have an inner vision of what you intend to manifest and still detach yourself from the outcome. How? Consider this observation in *A Course in Miracles*: "Infinite patience produces immediate results." It sounds like a paradox, doesn't it? Infinite patience implies an absolute certainty that what you'd like to manifest will indeed show up, in perfect order, and exactly on time. The immediate result you receive from this inner knowing is a sense of peace. When you detach from the outcome, you're at peace, and you'll ultimately see the fruits of your convictions.

Suppose you had a choice between two magic wands. With Wand A, you can have any physical thing you desire by simply waving it. With Wand B, you can have a sense of peace for the rest of your life regardless of what circumstances arise. Which would you pick? A guarantee of stuff, or inner peace for the remainder of your life? If you opt for peace, then you already have Wand B. Simply have a mind that is open to everything but attached to nothing. Let it all come and go as it will. Enjoy it all, but never make your happiness or success dependent on an attachment to any thing, any place, and particularly, any person.

In all of your relationships, if you can love someone enough to allow them to be exactly what they choose to be—without any expectations or attachments from you—you'll know true peace in your lifetime. True love means you love a person for what they are, not for what you think they should be. This is an open mind—and an absence of attachment.

DAY 3

Don't Die with Your Music Still in You

Kahlil Gibran said, "When you are born, your work is placed in your heart." So, what is your work? Are you living your life the way your heart urges you to? That's our topic for today.

The world you live in is an intelligent system in which every moving part is coordinated by every other moving part. There's a universal life force that supports and orchestrates everything. It all works together in perfect harmony. You are one of those moving parts. You showed up here in the body you inhabit, precisely on time. Your body will leave here with the same precision. You're an essential piece of this complex system. Here you are in this intelligent system that has no beginning and no end, in which all of the galaxies move in harmony with each other. You must have shown up here for a reason!

Listening to Your Heart

Take a moment right now and point to yourself. Your finger is very likely pointing right at your heart. Not at your brain, but your heart. This is who you are. The constant beating of your heart in and out, out and in, is a symbol of your infinite connection to the always-present heartbeat of God, or the Universal Intelligence. Your left brain calculates, figures things out, analyzes, and comes up with the most logical choices for you. It thinks, thinks, thinks! Your right brain represents your intuitive side. This is the part of you that goes beyond reason and analysis. It's the part of you that feels things, that's sensitive to love, that's emotional about what's important to you. Your right brain allows you to tear up as you hold your babies, or bask in the beauty of a glorious day. Your left brain can *analyze* it, while your right brain lets you *feel* it.

Pick a situation and ask yourself if what you know or what you feel is most important to you. Generally, what you'll take care of first depends on the situation and circumstances you're in. Your intellect can be figuring out exactly how you're supposed to act in a relationship when things are collapsing (or when they're rapturous), and then there are times when what you feel will supersede what you know. If you *are* feeling fearful, scared, lonely; or on the other hand, thrilled, loving, and ecstatic, these will be the dominant forces you'll act upon. These are the times when your right brain is right. Your right brain will always lead you passionately to your purpose.

Listening to Your Right Brain

There's an intuitive, invisible presence that's always with you. I picture this presence as a nagging little creature who sits on your right shoulder and reminds you when you've lost your sense of purpose. This little fellow is your own death, urging you to get on with what you showed up here for because you have only so many days to get it done, and then your body will be departing from this visit. Your invisible companion will prod you when you're spending another day doing what somebody else has dictated if it's not a part of your passion in life.

You'll most likely always know when you're off purpose because of your thoughts of frustration. You might not always act on this knowledge, though, because your left brain has not mustered up the courage to do the bidding that your right brain knows is your destiny. Your intuitive inner voice keeps urging you to play the music that you hear so that you won't die with it inside you. But your left brain says, "Wait a minute. Be careful, don't take risks, you might fail, you might disappoint all of those who have a different view of what you should be doing." Then your right-brain invisible companion (your death) speaks even louder. The volume gets turned up and up, trying to get you to follow your dream.

Listening exclusively to your left brain will turn you ultimately into a pretender, or even worse, a commuter—getting up every morning going with the crowd, doing that job that brings in the money and pays the bills; and getting up the next morning and doing it all over again, as a well-known song implies. Meanwhile, the music inside of you fades almost to a point of being inaudible. But your constant invisible companion always hears the music and continues tapping you on your shoulder.

The attempts to get your attention may take the form of an ulcer, or a fire to burn up your resistance, or being fired from a stifling job, or being brought to your knees with an accident. Usually these accidents, illnesses, and forms of bad luck finally get your attention. But not always. Some people end up like Leo Tolstoy's character Ivan Ilyich, who anguished on his deathbed, "What if my whole life has been wrong?" A fearsome scene, I must say.

You don't have to choose that fate. Follow your right brain, listening to how you feel, and play your own unique brand of music. You won't have to fear anything or anyone, and you'll never experience that terror of lying on your deathbed someday, wondering if your whole life has been wrong. Your invisible companion on your right shoulder will prod you each and every time you're moving away from your purpose. It makes you aware of your music. Listen to your invisible companion, express the music that you hear, and ignore what everyone else around you thinks you should be doing. As Henry David Thoreau put it, "If a man does not keep pace with his companions, perhaps it is because he hears a different drummer. Let him step to the music he hears, however measured or far away."

Be willing to accept that others may even see you as having betrayed them, but you haven't betrayed your music, your purpose. Do what you know you have to do to feel whole, to feel complete, and to feel as if you're fulfilling your destiny. You'll never be at peace if you don't get that music out and let it play. Don't die with that music still in you.

DAY 4

Being Passionate Means Taking Risks

As we saw yesterday, to fulfill your true destiny, you must follow your instincts. Of course, if you don't, you may still find yourself living a comfortable life— you pay your bills, fill out all of the right forms, and live a life of fitting in and doing it by the book. But it's a book that was written by somebody else. You're aware of that nagging companion saying to you, "This may look right, but does it feel right? Do you have a passion for your chosen path in life?" For many people, the answer is, "How do I discover my passion?" Today, I'm going to help you answer that question.

You'll find your passion in what inspires you the most. And what does the word "inspire" mean? It derives from the words "in spirit". When you're inspired, you never have to ask about your purpose. You're living it. For one of my children, it's about riding horses and being at the stables. She's in heaven when on horseback or even cleaning out a stall filled with horse manure. Another daughter is only inspired when she's singing, writing music, or performing. She's felt that way since she was two. For another, it's her artwork and design that make her feel purposeful. For yet another, it's designing websites and creating computer programs for others. For me, it's writing and speaking and creating products to help people become self-reliant. This has always been my passion, even as a young boy.

What is *your* passion? What stirs your soul and makes you feel like you're totally in harmony with why you showed up here in the first place? Know this for certain: Whatever it may be, you can make a living doing it and simultaneously provide a service for others. I guarantee it.

Being excited about life is infectious—it rubs off on others. I'm reminded of a whale-watching trip I took, where I observed a young woman I know named Beth as she spoke to a group of people about humpback whales. Her enthusiasm was palpable to the entire group aboard the boat, and the more passion she displayed, the more she seemed to inspire her audience. I've been aboard other boats and seen the impact of guides who merely go through the motions: People in this low-energy environment don't leave the experience feeling inspired.

Beth, on the other hand, feels a passion that she conveys to others every single day during the whale-mating season. Every day! You see, she studied marine biology in college and has always been fascinated by humpback whales and their amazing ability to travel between Alaska and Hawaii, to go six months without eating, to give birth in warm waters, and then navigate to cold waters on the return. For Beth, these whales are a part of God's mysterious, miraculous creation. She's living her passion, and she inspires others by her enthusiastic way of being. In fact, everyone in this vicinity knows that expeditions with Beth are almost a guarantee that you'll not only get to see the whales, but that they'll dance and breach and even swim under the boat for you. It's as if the whales themselves respond to Beth's excitement!

When you're enthusiastically living your passion, whatever it may be, you transmit spiritual signals to those around you that you're loving who you are, what you came here to be, and whoever comes into your field of vision.

The only thing that will keep you from your passion is fear. According to *A Course in Miracles*, there are only two basic emotions: One is fear, the other is love.

You may fear the disapproval of others. Take that risk and you'll discover that you receive more approval when you don't seek it than when you do. You may fear the unknown. Take that risk as well. Wander in there, asking yourself, "What is the worst thing that can happen if this doesn't work out?" The truth is that you will just move beyond it. You're not going to starve to death or be tortured if it doesn't work out. You might fear being successful. You may have been conditioned to believe you're inadequate or limited. The only way to challenge these absurdities is to go toward what you know you're here for and let success chase after you, as it most assuredly will. Or, you may fear the biggest one of all: You may fear failure.

The Myth of Failure

This may come as a surprise to you, but failure is an illusion. No one ever fails at anything. Everything you do produces a result. If you're trying to learn how to catch a ball and someone throws it to you and you drop it, you haven't failed. You simply produce a result. The real question is what you do with the results that you produce. Do you leave, and moan about being a failure, or do you say, "Throw it again," until ultimately you're catching balls? Failure is a judgment. It's just an opinion. It comes from your fears, which can be eliminated by love. Love for yourself. Love for what you do. Love for others. Love for your planet. When you have love within you, fear cannot survive. Think of the message in this ancient wisdom: "Fear knocked at the door. Love answered and no one was there."

That music that you hear inside of you urging you to take risks and follow your dreams is your intuitive connection to the purpose in your heart since birth. Be enthusiastic about all that you do. Have that passion with the awareness that the word "enthusiasm" literally means "the God (*enthos*) within (*iasm*)". The passion that you feel is God inside of you beckoning you to take the risk and be your own person.

I've found that perceived risks are not risky at all once you transcend your fears and let love and self-respect in. When you produce a result that others laugh at, you're also stirred to laughter. When you respect yourself, stumbling allows you to laugh at yourself as an occasional stumbler. When you love and respect yourself, someone's disapproval is not something you fear and avoid. The poet Rudyard Kipling declared, "If you can meet triumph and disaster, and treat those two imposters just the same... yours is the Earth and everything that's in it." The key word here is "imposters." They're not real. They exist only in the minds of people.

Let the world know why you're here, and do it with passion.

DAY 5

You Can't Give Away What You Don't Have

Of course you can't give away what you don't have! That seems so obvious that you may be wondering why I would mention it. It's because I've found that most people who don't enjoy inner peace and success in their lives have failed to master this simple truth. So today we are going to examine our own inner resources.

Think of the people you know who give love in response to negative energy that's directed their way. There aren't very many people who respond lovingly in that situation. The ones who do are able to because they have love to give away. They know that it's impossible to give away what they don't have, and they've gone that extra mile to acquire what it is that they want to both attract and give away. If love and joy are what you want to give and receive, then remember that you can't give away what you don't have, but you can change your life by changing what's inside if you're willing to go that extra mile.

Changing What's Inside

Consider the following concept of your inner reality. Your thoughts create your reality because your thoughts determine how you respond to situations in your daily life. Those responses are the energy you have inside of you to give away. If you feel anger, it's because you have anger energy in your body. Like everything in our universe, your thoughts are a form of energy. Everything that you feel and experience is the result of what I call "attractor energies." This means that you get back what you put out into the world. Thus, what you've attracted to you is what you have to give away to others.

Low energy attracts low energy. Some of the low energy thoughts are anger, hate, shame, guilt, and fear. Not only do they weaken you, but they attract more of the same! By changing your inner thoughts to the higher frequencies of love, harmony, kindness, peace, and joy, you'll attract more of the same, and you'll have those higher energies to give away. These higher and faster frequencies that empower you will automatically nullify and dissipate the lower energies in the same way that the presence of light makes darkness disappear.

Loving and Respecting Yourself

By becoming more loving toward yourself, you will attract more of the higher, faster energies and begin to change what's inside you. In your thoughts, cultivate an inner voice and attitude that's 100 percent of the time *for* you. Imagine an aspect of yourself that only supports and loves you. You might schedule a certain time of the day when that's the only thought that you allow yourself to pay attention to! Gradually this attitude will extend to other people even if you can only do it for a minute or two. You'll begin to receive this energy back and ultimately be able to send thoughts of love and joy to everyone and everything in your world. Notice when your thoughts drift into the lower energy of ridicule or hate or guilt, and change the thought at that very moment, if at all possible. If you're unable to change your thought, at least love yourself for what you *did* do—that is, for noticing.

Make a pact to remind yourself often of this secret of not being able to give away anything that you don't have. Then work on your personal program of self-love, self-respect, and self-empowerment, and create a huge inventory of what you wish to give away.

One of the lessons I continue to learn and practice is that the universe responds with the same energy that we send out. If you attract a lot of people who wish to take advantage of you, you need to consider what you're doing to attract victimizers into your life. If you run into anger a lot, explore the angry thoughts you have inside you. If your consciousness is a "Gimme! Gimme! Gimme!" energy, you'll attract all manner of demanding energies into your life. You know if this is true by the number of deadlines not being met, demanding bosses or customers you encounter, and the feeling of being a victim. Send out "Gimme! Gimme! Gimme!" energy to the universe, and it will do the same in return.

If what you give is self-respect and self-love, the universe, via the attractor energy, will return the love and respect you've been radiating. It's really so simple. You can't give away what you don't have.

The Irony of Giving

If you wanted to give a dozen oranges to your neighbor as an expression of love, you obviously would need to be in possession of 12 oranges. If you intended to purchase a new automobile for your parents to show your gratitude to them for putting you through medical school, naturally you'd need to have the funds to do so. Likewise, you can't give love away to others if you don't have any for yourself. You can't show respect for others if you lack self-respect. You can't give happiness away if you feel unhappy. And of course, the reverse is true.

You can only give away what you do have, and all that you're giving away each and every day are items from your own personal inventory. If you give away hatred, it's because you've stored up hatred inside of you to give away. If you give away misery, it's because you have a ready supply available from which to select and distribute.

This concept is simplified by a description of squeezing an orange. When you squeeze an orange, you'll always get orange juice to come out. This is true regardless of who does the squeezing, what time of day you squeeze, what instrument you use to squeeze, or what circumstances surround the orange-squeezing. What comes out is what's inside. The same logic applies to you.

When someone squeezes you, in some way puts pressure on you, or says something unflattering or critical; and out of you comes anger, hatred, bitterness, tension, depression, or anxiety, it's because that is what's inside. The irony is that you can't give away what you don't have because you're always giving what you do have. If you want to move into the realm of purpose by giving and serving others, ask yourself, "What do I have inside?" and "Why have I chosen to store these kinds of energies in me to give to others?"

DAY 6

Your Purpose Is to Serve

If you are like most people I meet, you most likely yearn to know your purpose in life. "How can I find my purpose?" is the question that I am asked most often. The questioner often elaborates on his or her dilemma by saying, "I would be happier if I could be living out my purpose, but I just don't know what my purpose in life is." My response is that you come into this world with absolutely nothing. You will leave this physical world with exactly the same. All of your acquisitions and achievements can't go with you. Therefore, the only thing you can do with your life is give it away. Today, we're going to discuss how to feel purposeful by discovering a way to always be in the service of others.

Purpose is about serving. It's about taking the focus off you and your self-interest, and serving others in some way. You build because you love to build. But you build to make others happy. You design because your heart directs you to. But those designs are in the service of others. You write because you love to express yourself in words. But those words will help and inspire readers. If you don't yet know your purpose, you'll continue to seek it throughout the various stages of your life.

There are many different models that describe the stages of life. Here, I'm using the four archetypal stages of athlete, warrior, statesman, and spirit to briefly show what your purpose is in each stage.

In the athlete archetype, the focus is exclusively on the physical body and how it looks and performs. The warrior archetype wants to compete, defeat, and collect the rewards. The statesman archetype emphasizes fulfilling the desires of others by asking,

"How may I serve?" At the final stage (and the highest that we know) is the archetype of spirit. At this stage, you realize what is meant by being *in* this world, but not *of* this world. The spirit part of you knows that neither the body nor this world is its exclusive domicile. This spirit archetype invites you to minimize your material-world concerns and to put more of your energy into the essence of life, which is love and service.

As you progress through these four archetypes, you'll find yourself thinking less and less of your own self-interest and more and more about how you can make the world a better place for all. In this way, you discover a great truth. The more you chase after your own goals and pursue your self-interest, the more these aims will elude you. But when you turn your thoughts and then your activities, regardless of what they are, to serving others, those things that you used to chase after will follow you wherever you go. When you get yourself out of the picture completely, the forces of the universe will seem to conspire to provide all that you previously sought for yourself. And then, because you're not attached to them any longer, they'll flow in and out of your life freely.

In essence, I'm urging you to stop taking your life so personally. You can end any and all suffering by reminding yourself that nothing in the universe is personal. Of course you've been taught to take life very personally, but this is an illusion. Tame your ego, and absolutely free yourself from ever taking anything personally.

One good way to serve is to practice being generous as often as you can. Promise yourself to extend some kind of unexpected generosity to someone, preferably a stranger, every single day for two weeks. This will not only help you develop a habit of giving, but you'll also discover how wonderfully inspiring your generous nature feels. The more you practice being charitable, the more you'll impact others and encourage them to help and serve others, too. By letting others know that you're willing to give your time as well as your possessions, you'll serve as a great role model. Who isn't inspired by those who are willing to share their time, money, and possessions? We name cities (San Francisco) for such people and we nominate them (Mother Teresa) for sainthood… you, too, can make a difference by being a benevolent soul.

You can also practice tithing (giving 10 percent of what you earn in a given period to support teaching that provides you with spiritual uplift) and see if it doesn't return to you tenfold. This has worked for me my entire life, and continues as I practice my natural instinct to be generous.

In an exceptional book titled *Season of Life*, Jeffrey Marx, a Pulitzer Prize-winning writer, chronicles a high school football team in which a former player with the Baltimore Colts named Joe Ehrmann is on the coaching staff. His coaching philosophy is to "help boys become men within the context of sports"— that is, without threats, screaming, or violence.

"I expect greatness out of you," the team's head coach tells his players, "and the way we measure greatness is the impact you make on other people's lives." As the 10 coaches and assistant coaches huddle with the team on game day, one of them asks, "What is our job?" "To love us!" the team yells back in unison. "And what is your job?" the coach asks. "To love each other," the team responds. This is the philosophy that these boys were exposed to every day—at practice, on the field, and during and after the games—and so it goes for all of us who wish to serve others. We must love all others and teach them to love each other.

Keep these thoughts in mind, particularly when you feel lost or are unsure of your purpose: "My purpose is about giving. I'll direct my thoughts off me, and spend the next few hours looking for a way to be of service to anyone or any creature on our endangered planet." This will bring you back to a realization that it doesn't matter what you do, as long as you're able to give. In order to fully give and be of service and ultimately feel purposeful, you must be able to say, "Yes," when you ask yourself, "Do I really possess what it is that I wish to give away?"

DAY 7

Embrace Silence

Today our topic is that rare commodity in 21st-century living—silence.

You live in a noisy world, constantly bombarded with loud music, sirens, construction equipment, jet airplanes, rumbling trucks, leaf blowers, lawn mowers, and tree cutters. These human-made, unnatural sounds invade your senses and keep silence at bay. In fact, you've been raised in a culture that not only eschews silence, but is terrified of it.

The car radio must always be on, and any pause in conversation is a moment of embarrassment that most people quickly fill with chatter. For many, being alone is a nightmare, and being alone in silence is pure torture. The famous scientist Blaise Pascal observed, "All man's miseries derive from not being able to sit quietly in a room alone."

The Value of Silence

There's a momentary silence in the space between your thoughts that you can become aware of with practice. In this silent space, you'll find the peace that you crave in your daily life. You'll never know that peace if you have no spaces between your thoughts. The average person is said to have 60,000 separate thoughts every day. With so many thoughts, there are almost no gaps. If you could reduce that number by half, you would open up an entire world of possibilities for yourself.

It's really the space between the notes that makes the music you enjoy so much. Without the spaces, all you would have is one continuous noisy note. Everything that's created comes out of silence. Your thoughts emerge from the nothingness of silence. Your words come out of this void. Your very essence emerged from emptiness. Those who will supersede us are waiting in the vast void. All creativity requires some stillness. Silence reduces fatigue and allows you to experience your own creative juices.

Accessing More Silence in Your Life

I urge you to demand more and more time for silence in your life. One of the most effective ways to bring this about is to make meditation a daily practice. And remember, there's no such thing as a bad meditation. Give yourself time to sit quietly alone. At first your thoughts will take off trying to convince you that this is a waste of time, that you should be out there being productive, and that you've got so many other things to do. Hundreds of other unrelated thoughts will pop in and out of your mind.

But you can weather this thunderstorm of mental protestations by sitting quietly and becoming the observer to all of this inner chatter. Eventually you'll be able to move to the gaps between your thoughts and notice how peaceful you felt in that silent gap when you emerge from it. Try it right now. Use the

Lord's Prayer. First, concentrate on the word *Our,* and then *Father.* Try to go into the gap between the two words, *Our* and *Father.* Then do it again with *Who art* and *in Heaven.* Just slip momentarily into the gap, and notice how peaceful and exquisite you feel in that gap.

There are many opportunities to access silence. I try to meditate each time I stop at a red light. With the car stopped and my body inactive, frequently the only things still moving are the thoughts in my mind. I use those two minutes or so at the stoplight to bring my mind into harmony with my inert car and body. I get a wonderful bonus of silence. I probably stop at a red light 20 or 30 times a day, creating 40 minutes to an hour of silence. And there's always someone behind me to let me know that my time is up by breaking the silence with a honking horn!

The Wilderness Is Therapy

Anytime in your life when you're feeling out of sorts in any way, go to nature and find silence and peace. Sending troubled teens to the wilderness to care for animals and commune with nature almost always brings them peace and serenity. Drug addictions disappear when young people are confronted with climbing a mountain or canoeing across a lake. People who have been diagnosed with terminal illnesses often find that months spent in a cabin in the isolated wilderness is the exact therapy they need, and sometimes the source of miraculous spontaneous remissions.

If you ever suffer from insomnia, walk barefoot on the grass for 10 minutes before getting into bed. Nature has a marvelous way of healing many maladies. Try spending a day in an isolated spot, listening only to silence punctuated by the sounds of nature—the birds, the insects, the rustling of leaves, the wind. These are the sounds of healing that can offset the painful sounds of trucks, cement mixers, boom boxes, and the like.

Give yourself opportunities to be in the wilderness as a regular part of your life routine. Take a day each month or week or two to be alone in silence, communing with nature. This is the ultimate therapy, and it's much less expensive than paying someone to listen!

Meditation Not Only Affects You, It Impacts Everyone Around You

When you're at peace, you radiate a different kind of energy than when you're stressed or depressed. The more peaceful you become, the easier you can deflect the negative energies of those you encounter. This is like having an invisible shield around you that nothing can penetrate unless it's at a higher spiritual energy than your shield. A hostile current is greeted with a smile and an inner knowing that this is not your stuff. A person who attempts to bring you into their misery cannot succeed without your agreement. Your meditation practice keeps you immune.

Not only can you deflect the negativity of those around you, but your sense of peace will bring others into harmony with you. Studies have been done to measure the serotonin (a neurotransmitter in your brain that indicates how peaceful and harmonious you feel) levels of those in the vicinity of a large group of meditators. Amazingly, just being in the energy field of those who meditate raises the serotonin levels of the observers. These implications are startling. The more you achieve peacefulness through meditation, the more your peaceful state impacts those around you.

I find that my meditating not only calms me, but has a soothing effect on my family and those around me. But the primary benefit is that after a meditation, I find it almost impossible to be annoyed or negatively impacted by anything, because it brings me inner peace.

DAY 8

Making Conscious Contact with God

Most organized religions have taken on the task of explaining God to their congregations, including all of the rules that God supposedly has laid out for humankind. However, you cannot come to know God through the experiences or testimony of others. This must be done by you. Today, through further exploration of meditation and silence, we are going to discover how to make conscious contact with God.

I teach a meditation, which I describe in detail and guide you through with my voice, in an audio program called *Meditations for Manifesting*. This meditation uses the sound of "ahhhh" as a mantra to keep your thoughts from wandering during the morning meditation. This mantra sound is in virtually all names of the Divine. Listen for it, for example, in *God*, *Yahweh*, *Allah*, *Krishna*, *Jehovah*, *Ra*, and *Ptah*. By repeating this mantra sound, you make conscious contact with God. The evening meditation uses the sound of *om*, the sound of gratitude for all that has manifested in your life. Repeating the sound of *ahhhh* in the morning and *om* in the evening for approximately 20 minutes creates an opportunity for you to experience inner peace and success, in a way you may have never known before. I urge you to meditate because it will bring you more peace, remove stress, improve your surroundings, and deflect negativity. All of this and more will definitely show up when you meditate on a regular basis.

When you merge into the silence and become one with it, you also reconnect to your Source and know the peacefulness that some call God. "Be still and know that I am God," says it so beautifully in the Psalms of the Old Testament. The key words here are *still* and *know*.

Be still actually means *silence*. Mother Teresa described silence and its relationship to God by saying, "God is the friend of silence. See how nature—trees, grass—grows in silence; see the stars, the moon, and the sun, how they move in silence... We need silence to be able to touch souls." This includes your soul!

The second word in the Old Testament observation, *know*, refers to making your personal and conscious contact with God. To know God is to banish doubt and become independent of others' definition and description of God. Instead, you have your own personal knowing. And as Herman Melville reminded us so poignantly, "God's one and only voice is silence."

Your sense of inner peace depends on spending some of your life energy in silence to recharge your battery, remove tension and anxiety, reacquaint you with the joy of knowing God, and feel closer to all of humanity.

The Divine Oneness

God is that which is indivisible. There's only one omnipresent presence called God. This presence is everywhere and is a force that creates and sustains life. It can never be divided or cut up into pieces. There's only one power in the universe, not two. Everything in your experience as a human being appears to be in duality, however. *Up* exists because of its opposite, *down. Light* exists because of *dark; right* exists because of *wrong.* You've never seen a person with a *front* who doesn't have a *back;* an *outside* without an *inside;* a *north pole* of a magnet without a *south pole.* Our physical world is a world of dichotomies and combinations of opposites, always divisible.

Silence, however, is the one experience you can have that's indivisible. You cut silence in half, and all you get is more silence. There's only one silence. Therefore, silence is your one way to experience the oneness and the indivisibility of God. This is how you *know God* rather than having to settle for *knowing about God.* This is why you want to meditate. Meditation seems to bring me into contact with a source of soothing energy that makes me feel deeply connected to God.

You will find your answers in the silence. Remember: It's out of the void, the emptiness, that everything is created. When you write a musical note, the silence from which it comes is just as much a part of the note as is the sound. So it is with healing any thing or any relationship. Going into the quiet and listening will inspire you. I can't imagine speaking or writing without first going to God in silence. I seek alone time and space to allow my inspiration to emerge.

Keep Your Silent Communion with God to Yourself

Everything that you wish to manifest emerges from Spirit, from the silence. You don't use your ego to manifest. In fact, ego can inhibit the creative process. For this reason, I urge you not to divulge your private insights, what you intend to create. As St. Paul said, "That which is seen, hath not come from that which doth appear." When you talk about your emerging manifesting ideas and relate your insights to others, you often feel the need to explain and defend them. What happens is that ego has entered. Once the ego is present, the manifesting stops.

Silence is where manifesting occurs, so keep your potential miracles in the treasured silence that you embrace as often as possible. You can rely upon it and enjoy basking in the serenity and inner peace that silence and meditation always bring.

DAY 9

Give Up Your Personal History

For many of us, our past defines who we are at this present moment. Today, I want to show you how letting go of the past can help you move on to live your life more fully in the present.

When a speedboat zooms across the surface of the water, there's a white foamy froth behind it that's called the *wake* of the boat. The wake is nothing more than the trail that's left behind. The answer to, "What is driving the boat?" is that the boat moves because of present-moment energy generated by the engine. This is what makes the boat move forward across the water. Do you think it's possible for the wake to drive the boat? Can the trail that's left behind make a boat go forward? These are rhetorical questions with obvious answers. I'm sure you agree that the wake is only the trail left behind, and that it's not what drives the boat forward.

I'm suggesting that you apply this idea to your life. The wake of your life is nothing more than a trail that's left behind you. Thought of in this way, it's absolutely impossible for that wake to drive you forward. The wake is not in any logical way responsible for what you're experiencing or failing to experience today. The wake is just what it is, and nothing more—a trail that you've left behind. But have you?

Being a Victim of Your Personal History

For well over a quarter century now, I've worked with people to help them access higher levels of awareness. It's my experience that most people live their life in the wake by hanging on to personal histories to justify their self-defeating behaviors and the scarcity in their lives. They hang on to past pains, abuses, and shortcomings as calling cards to announce a "poor me" status to everyone they meet, within minutes of their introduction. "I was abandoned as a child," "I'm an alcoholic," "I'm an incest survivor," "My parents were divorced and I've never gotten over it." The list could go on for hundreds of pages.

Your past is over! By bonding to your past, you not only ensure that you'll be immobilized today, but you prevent yourself from healing. By referring to past struggles and using them as the reasons for not getting on with your life today, you're doing the equivalent of attributing to the wake the ability to drive the boat. This also works in reverse. Many people refer to the good old days that are gone forever as the reason why they can't be happy and fulfilled today. "Everything has changed," "No one respects anyone else like they used to," "A dollar used to be worth a dollar, now everything is so overpriced," "People don't seem to want to help out like they did in the past," "When we were kids, we respected authority; today's kids walk all over their parents." This is also living in the wake and assigning responsibility to the past for why you can't be successful or happy today.

Getting Out of the Wake

Imagine a pencil with the ability to only write your past history. It has no use otherwise. All of your past is in that pencil. Are you going to keep it? What for? Are you going to give it up? Perhaps Omar Khayyam will inspire you with his poem:

> *The moving finger writes and having writ*
>   *moves on.*
> *Nor all thy piety nor wit can lure it back*
>   *to cancel half a line,*
> *Nor all thy tears wash out one word of it.*

You can cry all night about the history in that pencil, all that it contains, and all you wish you could erase— or bring back again—but all of your tears can't wash out one word of the past, as the poet-philosopher reminds you.

You want to let go of your personal history that's symbolized by that pencil, but when you walk away from it, no matter how far you walk, you look back and there it is. You're ready to be rid of your personal history and to more fully live in the present moment. But the pencil is always there when you look back. I suggest that you pick up the pencil, and with compassion, allow the words, wounds, and pain of the past to be written, embraced, examined, understood, accepted, and loved for all that you've learned and experienced. The act of picking it up and embracing it will give you the strength to transform the past into song, poem, paint, or ritual if you feel called to do those things, or to throw it away in your unique manner.

Embracing Your Personal History

In a universe that's an intelligent system with a Divine creative force supporting it, there simply can be no accidents. As tough as it is to acknowledge, you had to go through what you went through in order to get to where you are today, and the evidence is that you did. Every spiritual advance that you will make in your life will very likely be preceded by some kind of fall or seeming disaster. Those dark times, accidents, tough episodes, periods of impoverishment, illnesses, abuses, and broken dreams were all in order. They happened, so you can assume they *had* to and you can't *unhappen* them.

Embrace them from that perspective, with help if you need it, and then understand them, accept them, honor them, and finally retire and/or transform them in your own way. (I know someone who gives them a new job description.) Become free to immerse yourself in this moment—the *now* that's called the *present*—because it's simply that—a present to open, relish, nurture, play with, and enjoy and explore.

No Longer Relying on Your Past

Make an effort to remove all labels that you've placed on yourself. Labels serve to negate you. You must ultimately live up to the label rather than being the limitless spirit that is your true essence. You're not an American, an Italian, or an African. You're a member of one race, the human race. You're not a male or a female, a Democrat or a Republican. You are one with the true oneness, God. You are not athletic or magical, mathematical or literary, or any other label.

Transcending labels, particularly those that have been placed on you by others in your past, opens you to the opportunity of soaring in the now in any way that you desire.

Your past history and all of your hurts are no longer here in your physical reality. Don't allow them to be here in your mind, muddying your present moments. Your life is like a play with several acts. Some of the characters who enter have short roles to play, others, much larger. Some are villains and others are good guys. But all of them are necessary, otherwise they wouldn't be in the play. Embrace them all, and move on to the next act.

DAY 10

All You Get
Is Now

The past has gone, the future is still to come, so the present—the here-and-now—is all we have. This is our topic for today.

The willingness and ability to live fully in the now elude many people. While eating your appetizer, don't be concerned with dessert. While reading a book, notice where your thoughts are. While on vacation, be there instead of thinking about what should have been done and what has to be done when returning home. Don't let the elusive present moment get used up by thoughts that aren't in the here and now.

There's an irony to this habit of having your mind drift to other times and other places. You can only drift off in the now, because now is all you ever get. So drifting off is a way of using up your present moments. You do indeed have a past, but not now! And yes, you have a future, but not now! And you can consume your now with thoughts of "then" and "maybe", but that will keep you from the inner peace and success you could experience.

It's doubtful that other creatures waste the present in thoughts of past and future. A beaver only does beaver, and he does it right in the moment. He doesn't spend his days wishing he were a young beaver again, or ruminating over the fact that his beaver siblings received more attention, or his beaver father ran off with a younger beaver when he was growing up. He's always in the now. We can learn much from God's creatures about enjoying the present moment rather than using it up consumed with guilt over the past or worry about the future. Practice living in the moment, and refuse to allow any thoughts based on your past to define you.

Stop and take notice of all that's in your immediate space—the people, creatures, vegetation, cloud formations, building designs, everything. Stay in the present by meditating and getting closer to the ultimate now... God.

God Is Only Here Now

Think about this. God will not be doing anything different one hour from now than God is doing now. And God is not doing anything different now from what God was doing a thousand years ago. The truth is that you can only come to know God if you're willing to be at peace in the present moment.

Earlier, in Day 8, I discussed how meditation is a way of making conscious contact with God. Here, I would like to let you in on a sublime secret that I learned from one of my most influential teachers:

> *You will only come to truly know God when you give up the past and the future in your mind and merge totally into the now, because God is always here now.*

Very few people understand and live this principle, largely because of their conditioning and unwillingness to train their minds in present-moment living. That's one of the reasons why I sometimes say that "It's never crowded along the extra mile." On the extra mile, choosing inner peace and attracting success into your life while living in the present moment become a way of being.

So, make the commitment to live joyfully in the moment. Stop dreaming about the future and get back to the only thing any of us have: Now. Decide to live fully in the present, withdrawing attention from past and future. Your desire for inspiration activates the world of Spirit from which you came. Your imagined future, the stuff of goals, is an unnecessary way of squandering the present moment. *Be Here Now* is more than a great book title by Ram Dass, it's the essence of inspiration. Being in the now is the way to remove anxiety, stress, and even some illnesses.

As I sit here writing, I can daydream all I want about completing this book, but in reality, all I can really do (which is precisely what I *am* doing) is listen to my inner voice, offer a matching vibration to those inner pleadings, and feel the joy of allowing the thoughts to come through me onto the pages. The "goal" has been suspended in favor of being here now, living out what I'm being directed by my "Senior Partner" to do. The end result takes care of itself, particularly since I see the end result in my mind, and I use my present moments in harmony with that vision.

I recommend that you find a way to transform your past, and remind yourself as you do that you're transforming any and all beliefs that you've used as labels or indicators of your limitations. To empower yourself in the present, replace all that with a knowing that you're not what you've done, what you've been, how others have taught you, or what has been done to you—instead you're a part of the beloved, connected now and always to your Source, and therefore connected to the unlimited power of the beloved. You can be all things at any present moment in your life.

DAY 11

You Can't Solve a Problem with the Mindset That Created It

Today we are examining the topic of problems and how changing the way we think can solve them.

Any problem can be resolved with a spiritual solution. One of the most intriguing passages in *A Course in Miracles* suggests that you don't have a problem; you only think you do. The opening lines of the Torah, as well as Genesis in the Bible, state, "God created Heaven and Earth," and later, "And all that God created was good." If you interpret those words literally, it's quite clear that problems are impossible. If God created everything and all that God created was good, bad does not exist. "But," you say, "disease, disharmony, despair, and so on all appear to exist and run rampant in our world."

When we feel separated from our sacred center, it's easy to believe so strongly in the separation that we explain any unpleasantness as a problem. In the world of Spirit, or God, problems simply don't exist and aren't real. When your spiritual connection is weak, you move away from the world of Spirit, and problems come from your belief in separation. Your mind creates the illusion of separateness, and your body, influenced by your ego thoughts, takes on diseases. Our societies are the creation of our collective thoughts. They take on the same separation-sickness, and then we have what we call *social problems*. All of the so-called problems, however, represent a spiritual deficit that can be remedied with spiritual solutions. Think of it this way: If you change your *mind*, you will solve your problem. (I've written an entire book on this subject called *There Is a Spiritual Solution to Every Problem*.)

How to Go about Changing Your Mind

Can you accept the idea that it's your belief in your separation from God that creates the attitude that you label a problem? Can you explore this idea that what you're calling problems are all simply illusions, or mistakes of your intellect? If God is everywhere, there is no place that God is not; therefore, you have God with you at all times. You may believe otherwise. It is this belief system that creates your so-called problems. If you can bring truth to the presence of these illusions, they will dissolve—just as you know that three plus three equals six is true, and that three plus three equals 10 is untrue. By bringing truth to the presence of this arithmetic error, it simply dissolves.

So too will all of your beliefs that create "problems" in your mind dissolve when you bring the higher energy of truth to them. St. Francis of Assisi, in his famous prayer, beseeches us to change our mind to this thought: "Where there is hatred let me sow love." Light always dissolves darkness. Love always nullifies hate. Spirit always cancels problems. Problems exist as beliefs of your ego mind, which is unable to conceptualize an awareness of your spiritual mind, just as dark has no concept of light.

By actually rewriting your agreement with reality, you can change your mind and send away any perceived problem. Change your attitude toward yourself, and resolve to believe in your connectedness to the higher energy of God, even in the direst of circumstances. Turn anything that seems problematic over to your higher self, trusting that the "problem" is not what it seems to be. Rewrite your agreement about who you are and what you're capable of achieving.

Your New Agreement with Reality

Your thoughts are the source of virtually everything in your life. Every relationship that you're in is something that you carry around with you. If your relationship is lousy, it's because you think of it that way. The person you're in a relationship with isn't with you in this moment, or when you're at work, or when you're in the bathroom, but your thoughts about that person are always with you. The only way you can experience another person is in your thoughts.

You can't get behind their eyeballs and be them. You can only process them with your thoughts. If you look for what's wrong about them and store that negative image in your mind, then that's where your relationship exists. If you change your thoughts to what you love rather than to what you label as wrong, you've just changed your entire relationship. It went from lousy to great by your changing your mind!

Try to always remember that you carry every relationship around with you in your head. Robert Frost reminded us, "You love the things you love for what they are." When you forget this and process other people on the basis of what you think they should be, or what they used to be, or how they compare to what you are, then you've sent love away, and in your mind, the relationship has soured. You experience every thing and every one in your thoughts. Change your thoughts, and you change what you carry around in your head as problems.

The world is just the way it is. The economy is just as it should be. The people who are behaving "badly" in the world are doing what they're supposed to be doing. You can process it in any way that you choose. If you're filled with anger about all of those "problems", you are one more person who contributes to the pollution of anger.

Your desire to do something about the lowest energies will motivate you to be more loving, more feeling, and more peaceful. And in so doing, you may influence those who are the farthest removed from God to return to their Source. This new agreement with yourself to always stay connected to Spirit even when it seems to be the most difficult thing to do will allow whatever degree of perfect harmony that your body was designed for to proliferate. Turn "diseases" over to God, and treat your body to regular exercise, healthy food, large amounts of pure water, and plenty of rest to allow it to function as a container for Spirit to flow through.

Your new agreement with reality in which you've blended your physical self and your personality with your spiritual God-connected self will begin to radiate a higher energy of love and light. Wherever you go, others will experience the glow of your God consciousness, and disharmony and disorder and all manner of problems simply will not flourish in your presence. Become "an instrument of Thy peace," as St. Francis desires in the first line of his famous prayer. Move up the ladder of human awareness from the lowest to the highest. Become a mystical being by simply changing your mind from one that created and experienced problems, to one that resolves them.

DAY 12

The Three Levels of Consciousness

We saw yesterday how changing our mindset and increasing our human awareness can help us to resolve problems. Today I'd like to introduce you to the three levels of consciousness, which will help you to gauge where you are on the ladder of awareness.

Throughout your life, you can measure yourself on the following three levels of consciousness. Few, if any of us, ever stay at any one level all of the time. These levels of awareness are presented from lowest to highest.

1. **The first level is ego consciousness.** In ego consciousness, your primary emphasis is on your personality and your body. There's an exceptionally strong belief in your separateness from everyone else, from all that you'd like to attract into your life, and from God. This attitude puts you into a state of competing for your share as if your job is to get there first. Winning and being number one seem to be the most important things you can do when you live at the level of ego consciousness. You spend a lot of your time measuring your success on the basis of how you stack up against others.

If you have more than others, you feel better about yourself. Having more money makes you feel better. Accumulating more awards and prestige and climbing higher on the corporate ladder encourage you to feel good about yourself. Ego consciousness prods you to compete, compare, and conclude that you are the best, so you concentrate on running faster and looking better than others. It's at this level of consciousness that problems exist. This is where inner peace is virtually impossible and success eludes you, because you must always be striving to be someplace else.

In order to walk comfortably along the extra mile, you must tame this ever-demanding, impossible-to-satisfy ego. Feelings of despair, anger, hatred, bitterness, stress, and depression stem from the ego's anxiety and insistence on living up to an external standard. The result is the anguish of not measuring up or fitting in properly. The ego will seldom allow you to rest, and demands more and more because it's terrified that you'll be called a failure. When you move beyond ego and make your higher self the dominant force in your life, you'll begin to feel that contentment and inner glow of peace and success that characterize the extra mile.

2. **The second level is group consciousness.** Group consciousness is very similar to ego consciousness with the exception that you move past yourself as the central focus of your life, and you now include others who are members of your group or your clan. You suppress your individual

ego and join a larger organization, the group ego. Your membership is based upon your family, your heritage, your racial background, your religion, your language, your political affiliation, and so on. You're required to think and act like the group to which you've been assigned.

At the group consciousness level, you're often dedicated to continuing social problems such as war, brutality, and religious persecution, which originated in ancestral enmities that have existed for thousands of years. But it also comes right down to daily living. Families insist that you adopt their viewpoint, hate whom they hate, and love whom they love.

You have blind allegiance to a company that may be making weapons of destruction, a concept to which you're normally opposed, but you do it anyway because "It's my job." Some policemen and soldiers victimize their fellow human beings by behaving worse than the criminals or so-called enemies they abhor so much. Our inhumanity to our fellow human beings is often justified on the grounds of a group-consciousness mentality. Members of gangs or societies will behave in horrid ways, spurred on by a group or clan mentality. In short, what the group dictates becomes your identification card as a human being.

Remember that, as we discussed yesterday, you can't solve any problem with the same mind that created it. In order to resolve a struggle that results from group consciousness, you have to change your mind or continue to have the problem haunt you. Resolving problems related to group consciousness involves moving into the highest level.

3. **The third level is mystical consciousness.** This level of problem-free consciousness is distinguished by the feeling of connectedness rather than separateness. At the level of mystical consciousness, you feel connected to every individual, every creature, the entire planet, and God.

Feeling connected means you truly sense that we are all one, and that harm directed at others is really harm directed at ourselves. Here, cooperation supplants competition; hatred is dissolved with love; and sadness is reduced to nothingness with joy. At this level, you're a member of the human race, not a sub-group. Here, you're a nation of the world with a global awareness, rather than a patriot of any one country. In mystical consciousness, you won't feel separate from any one, any thing, or God. You won't be what you have, what you accomplish, or what others think of you. You will be the beloved, and you will have changed your mind! Problems will now be only illusions of the mind that you no longer carry around with you.

As the great humanitarian Mahatma Gandhi put it, "Man becomes great exactly in the degree to which he works for the welfare of his fellow man." This is the level of mystical or God consciousness. It is a place where you can live a problem-free existence by changing your thoughts from ego and group consciousness to the higher level of mysticism. Here, you truly understand what Thoreau meant when he said, "There is no remedy for love but to love more."

DAY 13

There Are
No Justified
Resentments

You hear people say this all the time: "I have a right to be upset because of the way I've been treated. I have a right to be angry, hurt, depressed, sad, and resentful." Learning to avoid this kind of thinking is one of my top recommendations for living a life of inner peace, success, and happiness. Anytime you're filled with resentment, you're turning the controls of your emotional life over to others to manipulate. Today's topic is taking responsibility for everything (and I mean *everything*) in your life.

I became aware of how powerful this lesson was many years ago while sitting in on a meeting of 12 people who were in a recovery group for alcoholism and drug addiction. All 12 of those people were accustomed to blaming others for their weaknesses, using almost any excuse as a rationale for returning to their self-defeating ways. On a poster hanging in the room were these words: "In this group, there are no justified resentments."

Regardless of what anyone would say to another group member, no matter how confrontational or ugly the accusations, each person was reminded that there are no justified resentments. You may need to consider whom you resent before you can make your own choice about whether this is useful for you. Resentments give you an excuse to return to your old ways. This is what got you there in the first place!

Why Resentments Are There

You may be familiar with a popular television show called *Who Wants to Be a Millionaire?* If the contestant correctly answers 15 multiple-choice questions, he or she wins a million dollars. Starting with a $100 question, the person in the "hot seat" answers five questions before reaching the $1,000 level. At this point, the person is guaranteed to leave with something. Then the questions increase in difficulty. If the contestant reaches $32,000, again, there is a guarantee of leaving with that amount. So, there are two crucial levels to attain: The $1,000 level, which is achieved by answering five relatively simple questions; and the $32,000 level, which involves five increasingly difficult questions.

I've just related details about this TV program to present the idea of the two levels that you must achieve in order to have a chance at the highest "million-dollar" level of awareness. The $1,000 level is one in which you learn to leave blame behind in your life. If you don't do so, you go home with nothing.

Removing blame means never assigning responsibility to anyone for what you're experiencing. It means that you're willing to say, "I may not understand *why* I feel this way, why I have this illness, why I've been victimized, or why I had this accident, but I'm willing to say without any guilt or resentment that I own it. I live with it and I am responsible for having it in my life." Why do this? If you take responsibility for having it, then at least you have a chance to also take responsibility for removing it or learning from it.

If you're in some small (perhaps unknown) way responsible for that migraine headache or that depressed feeling, then you can go to work to remove it or discover what its message is for you. If, on the other hand, someone or something else is responsible in your mind, then of course you'll have to wait until *they* change for *you* to get better. And that is unlikely to occur. So, at the $1,000 level, blame has to go. Otherwise you go home with nothing and are unable to participate at the higher levels.

You must be willing to pass a new test at the second critical level, the $32,000 question, which is the final obstacle you must face in order to move into the more exalted realm of self-actualization and higher consciousness, the million-dollar spiritual level. At this level, you must be willing to send the higher, faster energies of love, peace, joy, forgiveness, and kindness as your response to whatever comes your way. This is the start of the uncrowded extra mile where you have only love to give away.

Someone says something to you that you find disagreeable, and rather than opting for resentment, you are able to depersonalize what you've just heard and respond with kindness. You would rather be kind than right. You have no need to make others wrong or to retaliate when you've been wronged. You do this for yourself. There is a Chinese proverb, "If you're going to pursue revenge, you'd better dig two graves." Your resentments will destroy you. They are low energies. And along the extra mile, you'll only meet others who have fully grasped this concept. The ones who haven't made it to this level are all back with the crowd who went out of the game long ago on an easier question, and most are still back there wondering why they keep going home with nothing! But I can assure you that they continue to blame others for their emptiness.

First, you have to get past blame. Then you have to learn to send love to all, rather than anger and resentment. The story is told of the enlightened master who always responded to outbursts of criticism, judgment, and ridicule with love, kindness, and peace. One of his devotees asked him how he could possibly be so kind and peaceful in the face of such disparaging invective. His response to the devotee was this question: "If someone offers you a gift, and you do not accept that gift, to whom does the gift belong?" Ask yourself, "Why would I allow something that belongs to someone else to be a source of my resentment?" As the title of a popular book says, "What you think of me is none of my business." Indeed, there are no justified resentments if you wish to walk along the extra mile and enjoy inner peace and success on every step of the path.

DAY 14

Stop Looking for Occasions to Be Offended

When you live at or below ordinary levels of awareness, you spend a great deal of time and energy finding opportunities to be offended. Today we're going to examine how you can stop allowing yourself to be offended by others and instead respond positively with love and forgiveness.

A news report, an economic downturn, a rude stranger, a fashion miscue, someone cursing, a sneeze, a black cloud, any cloud, an absence of clouds— just about anything will do if you're looking for an occasion to be offended. Along the extra mile, you'll never find anyone engaging in such absurdities.

Become a person who refuses to be offended by any one, any thing, or any set of circumstances. If something takes place and you disapprove, by all means state what you feel from your heart; and if possible, work to eliminate it and then let it go. Most people operate from the ego and really need to be right. So, when you encounter someone saying things that you find inappropriate, or when you know they're wrong, wrong, wrong, forget your need to be right and instead say, "You're right about that!" Those words will end potential conflict and free you from being offended. Your desire is to be peaceful—not to be right, hurt, angry, or resentful. If you have enough faith in your own beliefs, you'll find that it's impossible to be offended by the beliefs and conduct of others.

Not being offended is a way of saying, "I have control over how I'm going to feel, and I choose to feel peaceful regardless of what I observe going on." When you feel offended, you're practicing judgment.

You judge someone else to be stupid, insensitive, rude, arrogant, inconsiderate, or foolish, and then you find yourself upset and offended by their conduct. What you may not realize is that when you judge another person, you do not define them. You define yourself as someone who needs to judge others.

Just as no one can define you with their judgments, neither do you have the privilege of defining others. When you stop judging and simply become an observer, you will know the inner peace I'm writing about here. With that sense of inner peace, you'll find yourself free of the negative energy of resentment, and you'll be able to live a life of contentment. A bonus is that you'll find that others are much more attracted to you. A peaceful person attracts peaceful energy. You won't know God unless you're at peace, because God *is* peace.

Your resentments literally send God out of your life while you're busy being offended. Not being offended will mean eliminating all variations of the following sentence from your repertoire of available thoughts: "If only you were more like me, then I wouldn't have to be upset right now." You are the way you are, and so are those around you. Most likely, they will never be just like you. So stop expecting those who are different to be what you think they should be. It's never going to happen.

It's your ego that demands that the world and all the people in it be as you think they should be. Your higher sacred self refuses to be anything but peaceful, and sees the world as it is, not as your ego would like it to be. When you respond with hatred to hate directed at you, you've become part of the problem, which is hatred, rather than part of the solution, which is love. Love is without resentment, and readily offers forgiveness. Love and forgiveness will inspire you to work at what you are *for* rather than what you are against. If you're against violence and hatred, you'll fight it with your own brand of violence and hatred. If you're *for* love and peace, you'll bring those energies to the presence of violence, and ultimately dissolve the hatred. When Mother Teresa was asked to march against the war in Vietnam, she replied, "No, I won't, but when you have a march for peace, I'll be there."

A Final Word about Forgiveness and Resentment

At the root of virtually all spiritual practices is the notion of forgiveness. This was what came out of Jesus of Nazareth while he was being tortured on a cross by a Roman soldier throwing a spear into his side. It is perhaps the most healing thing that you can do to remove the low energies of resentment and revenge from your life completely.

Think about every single person who has ever harmed you, cheated you, defrauded you, or said unkind things about you. Your experience of them is nothing more than a thought that you carry around with you. These thoughts of resentment, anger, and hatred represent slow, debilitating energies that will disempower you. If you could release them, you would know more peace.

You practice forgiveness for two reasons. One is to let others know that you no longer wish to be in a state of hostility with that person; and two, to free yourself from the self-defeating energy of resentment.

Resentment is like venom that continues to pour through your system, doing its poisonous damage long after being bitten by the snake. It's not the bite that kills you; it's the venom. You can remove venom by making a decision to let go of resentments. Send love in some form to those you feel have wronged you and notice how much better you feel, how much more peace you have. It was one act of profound forgiveness toward my own father, whom I never saw or talked to, that turned my life around from one of ordinary awareness, to one of higher consciousness, achievement, and success beyond anything I had ever dared to imagine.

DAY 15

Treat Yourself as If You Already Are What You'd Like to Be

Whatever it is that you envision for yourself—no matter how lofty or impossible it may seem to you right now—I encourage you to begin acting as if what you would like to become is already your reality. This is our topic for today, and it's a wonderful way to set into motion the forces that will collaborate with you to make your dreams come true.

To activate the creative forces that lie dormant in your life, you must go to the unseen world, the world beyond your form. Here is where what doesn't exist for you in your world of form will be created. You might think of it in this way: In form, you receive *in-formation.* When you move to Spirit, you receive *in-spiration.* It is this world of inspiration that will guide you to access anything that you would like to have in your life.

What It Means to Become Inspired

Some of the most significant advice I've ever read was written more than 2,000 years ago by an ancient teacher named Patanjali. He instructed his devotees to become inspired. You may recall that the word "inspire" originates from the words "in" and "spirit." Patanjali suggested that inspiration involves a mind that transcends all limitations, thoughts that break all their bonds, and a consciousness that expands in every direction. Here is how you can become inspired.

Place your thoughts on what it is you'd like to become—an artist, a musician, a computer programmer, a dentist, or whatever. In your thoughts, begin to picture yourself having the skills to do these things. No doubts. Only a knowing. Then begin acting as if these things were already your reality. As an artist, your vision allows you to draw, to visit art museums, to talk with famous artists, and to immerse yourself in the art world. In other words, you begin to *act* as an artist in all aspects of your life. In this way, you're getting out in front of yourself and taking charge of your own destiny at the same time that you're cultivating inspiration.

The more you see yourself as what you'd like to become, the more inspired you are. The dormant forces that Patanjali described come alive, and you discover that you're a greater person than you ever dreamed yourself to be. Imagine that—dormant forces that were dead or non-existent, springing into being and collaborating with you as a result of your becoming inspired and acting as if what you want is already here!

By having the courage to declare yourself as already being where you want to be, you will almost force yourself to act in a new, exciting, and spiritual fashion. You can also apply this principle to areas other than your chosen vocation. If you're living a life of scarcity, and all of the nice things that many people have are not coming your way, perhaps it's time to change your thinking and act as if what you enjoy having is already here.

Visualize the beautiful automobile that's your dream car and paste it on your bedroom door, as well as on the refrigerator. While you're at it, paste it on the dashboard of the car you're now driving! Visit a showroom, sit in your car, and note the beautiful new-car aroma. Run your hands over the seats, and grip the steering wheel. Walk all around your car, appreciating the lines of it. Take your car for a test drive, and visualize that you're entitled to drive this car, that you're inspired by its beauty, and that it's going to find a way into your life. In some way, somehow, this is your car. Talk to others about your love for this car. Read about it. Bring up a picture on your computer screen, and leave it there to view each time you're near that computer.

All of this may seem silly to you, but when you become inspired and act as if what you want is already here, you'll activate those dormant forces that will collaborate to make this your reality.

Extending Inspiration Everywhere

Treating yourself in the manner described above can become a habitual way of life. This doesn't involve deception, arrogance, or hurting others. This is a silent agreement between you and God in which you discreetly work in harmony with the forces of the universe to make your dreams become a reality. This involves a knowing on your part that success and inner peace are your birthright; that you are a child of God; and as such, you are entitled to a life of joy, love, and happiness.

In your relationships with your lovers, co-workers, and family, act as if what you would like to materialize in these relationships is already here. If you want a sense of harmony in the workplace, maintain a clear vision and expectation of this harmony. Then, you're out in front of your day, seeing 5 p.m. arriving peacefully for everyone when it's still 7:30 a.m. Each time you have an encounter with someone, your 5 p.m. vision pops into your head, and you act in a peaceful, harmonious way so as not to nullify what you know is coming. Furthermore, you act toward everyone else as if they, too, are all that they are capable of becoming.

These kinds of expectations lead you to say, "I'm sure you'll have everything ready this afternoon," rather than, "You're always late with everything, and I wish you would get on the ball." When you treat others in this way, they also fulfill the destiny that you've reminded them is there for them.

In your family, particularly with your children, it's important to always have this little thought in mind: *Catch them doing things right.* Remind them often of their inherent brilliance, their capacity for being responsible, their innate talents, and their fantastic abilities. Treat them as if they're already responsible, bright, attractive, and honorable. "You are so terrific. I'm positive you'll feel great about your interview." "You're so smart, I know you'll study and do well on that exam." "You are always connected to God, and God doesn't do sickness. You're going to feel much better tomorrow at this time."

When you act toward your children, parents, siblings, and even more distant relatives as if the relationship is great and going to stay that way, and you point out their greatness rather than their goofiness, it is their greatness that you will see. In your relationship to your significant other, whoever that may be, be sure to apply this principle as frequently as you can. If things aren't going well, ask yourself, "Am I treating this relationship as it is, or as I would like it to be?" So how do you want it to be? Peaceful? Harmonious? Mutually satisfying? Respectful? Loving? Of course you do. As such, before your next encounter, see it in those ways. Have expectations that focus on the qualities of inner peace and success.

You'll find yourself pointing out what you love about that person rather than what they're doing wrong. You'll also see the other person responding to you in love and harmony rather than in an embittered way. Your ability to get out in front of yourself and see the outcome before it transpires will cause you to act in ways that bring about these results.

This strategy for living works for virtually everything. Before I speak to an audience, I always see them as loving, supportive, and having a terrific experience. Before writing, I see myself with no writer's block, being inspired and having spiritual guidance available to me at all times. As *A Course in Miracles* reminds us, "If you knew who walked beside you at all times, you could never experience fear again." This is the essence of inspiration, as well as seeing the future in terms of how you want it to be—and then acting exactly in that manner.

DAY 16

Synchronicity and Inspiration

There are no coincidences. Anything that coincides is said to fit together powerfully. You move into Spirit and feel inspired when you're activating the forces of the universe to work with you. Today we are looking at synchronicity and inspiration.

Since all is guided by Spirit, there is less of a gap between your thoughts and seeing the result of those thoughts materialize for you. As you place more and more of your energy on what you intend to manifest, you start seeing those intentions materializing.

You'll think about a particular person, and that individual will "mysteriously" appear. You'll need a book for your studies that you can't find, and it will show up in a "mysterious" delivery. You'll have in mind that you want information on a vacation spot, and it will arrive in the mail "mysteriously". All of these so-called mysteries will soon be viewed by you as part of the synchronicity of the universe working with you and your highly energized thoughts.

You must hold on to the idea that you can negotiate the presence of these things by keeping your energy field always focused with love on what you passionately intend to create. The Law of Attraction is put into play, and your thoughts literally become attractor energies. At first, it will seem startling and almost unbelievable. As you stay in Spirit and act as if what you desire is already here, you'll find it less and less puzzling.

Connected to God as you always are, you are the Divine force that puts this synchronicity into your everyday life. You will realize very soon that what you think about is what expands; therefore, you'll become more mindful and careful of what you think about. This process of treating yourself "as if" begins with your thoughts, impacts your emotional state, and finally stirs you into action.

Treat everyone you encounter with good intentions. Celebrate in others their finest qualities. Treat them all in this "as if" manner, and I guarantee you that they will respond accordingly to your highest expectations. It's all up to you. Whether you think this is possible or impossible, either way you'll be right. And you'll see the rightness of your thoughts manifesting everywhere you go.

From thoughts to feelings to actions, they will all react affirmatively when you stay inspired and get out in front of yourself in ways that are consistent with what you want to become. Declare yourself to be a genius, to be an expert, to be in an atmosphere of abundance, and keep that vision so passionately that you can do nothing but act upon it. As you do, you will send out the attractor energy that will work with you to materialize your actions based upon those stated declarations.

Small steps will activate matching vibrations to what you desire. So if you want to live close to nature, plan a visit to the place of your dreams and take the small steps to experience what it feels like. If you can't or won't do that, or if you aren't ready to go yet, you can read books or rent movies in order to have the experience vicariously. But be alert to the vibrational energy of thought and action that you offer Spirit.

When my daughter Skye wanted to produce an album of her own compositions, it seemed like a daunting task to write, perform, record, and arrange for all of the studio time and musicians. She continued to shy away from what inspired her, so I encouraged her to take a small step and write just one song. I gave her a suggestion for a title and a deadline—and then I watched with joy and pride as she sat at her piano, engrossed in her inspiration, creating. One small step put her on the path of inspiration, as Napoleon Hill suggested when he said, "If you can't do great things, do small things in a great way. Don't wait for great opportunities. Seize common, everyday ones and make them great."

Your Desires Don't Arrive by Your Schedule

Remember that all you desire will arrive in your life when and only when you're aligned vibrationally with the energy of your Source. Your ego won't be consulted or get to determine the schedule—God reveals His secrets when He is good and ready. Your job is to take the focus off the *when* and put it on being connected to your originating Spirit. Your job is to stop challenging and demanding responses from God, and instead be more like Him. Your job is to understand and accept that all of the things that show up in your life, which you often find contradictory or troublesome, are there because you've attracted them... and you need to have these obstacles in order to clear an opening for your true Spirit purpose to emerge.

So rather than making demands of God to follow your schedule, you can let go, surrender, and remind yourself that all is in Divine order. You're much more successful when you allow inspiration to flow in on God's terms than when you're impatient and demanding. As always, your job in God-realization is to become more like God—that means surrendering to the timetable that's always perfect, even when it seems to you to be full of errors.

DAY 17

Inspire Others

Just as we're all students throughout life, we're all teachers. In fact, we learn best by offering what we desire for ourselves to as many individuals as we can, as frequently as we can. So, it's imperative that we make a deliberate effort to increase our inspirational energy, as this will lead us to being both a spiritual learner and teacher simultaneously. Today we are exploring ways to inspire others.

Spiritual teachers have raised the vibrational frequency of their daily life to a point where they're able to provide inspiration to others merely by their presence, and this is the standard to which you need to aspire. It isn't necessarily a scholarly undertaking—

there are no lesson plans or report cards for the kind of teaching I'm writing about in these pages. Rather, I'm talking about the things you can do each and every day to inspire your fellow humans.

Act with Kindness

You can be on the lookout for opportunities to be a source of inspiration. For example, when I board an airplane, I tend to look for the chance to extend some sort of service to "strangers." (I put the word in quotes to emphasize that there aren't actually any strangers anywhere in the universe.) Helping vertically challenged passengers place their carry-on luggage in the overhead compartment is perfect because others noticing this act of kindness may be inspired, while, at the same time, I'm heeding my own calling to be both inspired and inspiring.

I know that someone who needs my assistance is really a Divine emissary who's right there in front of me, offering an opportunity for me to be in-Spirit. For instance, I flew from Maui to Los Angeles and then boarded an all-night flight to New York. On the way to L.A., I'd watched the fabulous movie *Chicago*; once on the plane to New York, I noticed one of the stars of that film, Renée Zellweger, getting on. Vertically challenged with heavy luggage, she certainly met all of my criteria for being both a source of inspiration and becoming inspired. I helped her with her baggage and then gave her a copy of one of my books.

Many people on the plane approached her, including the flight attendants, and I watched and felt inspired by the kindness, patience, and personal concern Renée showed toward everyone she talked to. As we left the plane, she handed me a note thanking me for both the book and my help. Whenever I see Renée in a movie or an interview, I recall the extraordinary, gentle kindness that she displayed toward everyone who approached her, and it inspires me. My moment or two of extending service to her was a gift to me, not because she's a celebrity, but because of that dual reward of being in-Spirit.

The Power of Gratitude

Without exception, I begin every day of my life with an expression of gratitude. As I look in the mirror to begin my daily ritual of shaving, I say, "Thank you, God, for life, for my body, for my family and loved ones, for this day, and for the opportunity to be of service. Thank you, thank you, thank you!"

If you practice gratitude as opposed to maintaining an attitude of entitlement, you'll automatically extend inspiration wherever you go. Being grateful helps remove the influence of your ego, which is certain that you're better than everyone else. An attitude of gratitude allows you to adopt what's called "radical humility," a trait that's very persuasive in helping others feel inspired.

Most of the people I've met or observed who are at the top levels in their chosen fields have these attitudes of gratitude and radical humility. After all, when so many high achievers reach for their statuette or championship trophy, they say, "First I'd like to thank God." It's almost as if they can't help themselves—they're so grateful for their accolade, but even more than that, they know that there's a Force in the universe way bigger than they are that allows them to act, sing, write, compete, or design. And if you adopt this kind of an attitude, you'll inspire others. It's that simple.

Pomposity, on the other hand, will never inspire anyone. When you encounter someone who brags and uses the pronoun "I" excessively, you'll find that you want to get away from them as quickly as possible. Vanity, conceit, and boasting are all signs that a person has edged God out of the picture.

Gratitude and humility send signals to all who meet and greet you that you're connected to something larger than life itself. This reminds me of the wisdom I discovered many years ago reading the *Kena Upanishad*: "At whose bequest does the mind think? Who bids the body live? Who makes the tongue speak? Who is the effulgent Being that directs eye to form and color, and the ear to sound?" When you know the answer to these questions, you not only become inspiring beings to others, you also gain immortality.

Being at Peace Inspires Others

Lecturing or demanding that others live peacefully is one of the least effective ways to inspire them; however, when you simply demonstrate that you're living peacefully, you offer other people a large dose of inspiration by your mere presence.

During my first encounter with Swami Satchidananda, for instance, he emitted such an aura of peacefulness that I felt inspired by merely standing next to him. It would have been impossible for me to feel anything other than peace in his midst. That day I purchased his wonderful book *Beyond Words*, and on page 21 was given an inkling as to why I felt so inspired merely by being in his company: "If anybody asks me, 'What is your philosophy of God?' I say, 'Peace is my God.' If they ask, 'Where is He?' I reply, 'He is in me and He is everywhere. He is all peaceful; He is all serenity. He is to be felt and experienced within oneself.'"

Being at peace with yourself is a way of going through life eschewing conflict and confrontation. When you're in a state of tranquility, you actually send out a vibration of energy that impacts all living creatures, including plants, animals, and all people (even babies). And, of course, the reverse applies as well: Belligerent individuals who live in turmoil and revel in hostile encounters send out nonverbal energy that adversely impacts those around them. The immediate impulse is to remove yourself from these low-energy, non-peaceful people because sticking around means tension and a lowering of your energy. Moreover, you become a counterforce to what you're experiencing, meaning that you become angry at their anger and arrogant toward their arrogance.

Practicing a peaceful approach to your life on Earth is a way of returning to where you came from. At the same time, it's a powerful source of inspiration to all living creatures.

DAY 18

Treasure
Your Divinity

You are a Divine creation of God. Today it is time to explore and value your own divinity.

You can never be separate from that which created you. If you can think of God as the ocean and yourself as a container, you may find it helpful in moments of doubt, or when you feel lost or alone, to remember that you are a container of God. When you dip your glass into the ocean, what you have is a glass of God. It's not as big or as strong, but it's still God. As long as you refuse to believe otherwise, you won't feel separate from God.

Think of a drop of water from the ocean of abundance that's separated from its source. Separated from its source, that droplet of water will ultimately evaporate and return to its source. The point is that while it's in liquid form, disconnected from its source, it loses the power of its source. This is the essence of the secret of always treasuring your divinity.

While you're separated in your mind from your Source, you lose your Divine power, the power of your Source. Just like the drop of water, you too will change form and ultimately return to your Source. As long as you feel disconnected from God, you lose the power of your Source, which is the unlimited power to create, to be miraculous, and to experience the joy of being alive. The drop of water, disconnected from its Divine Source, symbolizes your ego.

What Is Your Ego?

Your ego is nothing more than an idea that you carry around with you everywhere you go. This idea tells you that you are the sum total of what you have, what you do, and who you are. Ego insists that you are a separate being, that your personality and your body are your essence, and that you are in competition with every other ego to get your share of the pie, which is limited and finite. Therefore, ego asserts, you must be wary of others who also want all that they feel they're entitled to. Consequently, ego leads you to believe that there are enemies to be wary of at all times. Since you're separate from them, you must disdain cooperating with them for fear of being cheated. The result is that you have to distrust everyone!

Your ego also tells you that you're separate from everything that's missing in your life, and so you must spend a great deal of energy chasing after what's missing. Moreover, because who you are according to ego is your body and your personality, you're separate from God. God is outside of you, a force to fear just like all of those external forces attempting to control you. So you beg this external force to provide you with special powers to overcome all of those other egos who are trying so hard to snare what is rightfully yours.

Your ego keeps you in a constant state of fear, worry, anxiety, and stress. It implores you to be better than everyone around you. It beseeches you to push harder, and to get God on your side. In short, it maintains your separate status from God and allows you to be terrified of your own divinity.

Embracing Your Divinity

There is no place that God is not. Remind yourself of this every day. It has been said that God sleeps in the minerals, rests in the vegetables, walks in the animals, and thinks in us. Think of God as a presence rather than a person—a presence that allows a seed to sprout, that moves the stars across the sky, and simultaneously moves a thought across your mind. A presence that grows the grass and grows your fingernails all at the same time. This presence is everywhere; therefore, it must also be in you! And if it's everywhere, it must be in all that you perceive to be missing from your life. In some inexplicable way, you're already connected to all that you'd like to attract into your life by the presence of this universal, all-powerful Spirit called God.

You may have read about some of the great saints in India. They seem to possess the magical powers of instant manifestation, their presence appears to heal the sick, and they communicate a sense of divine bliss and peace to all those they encounter. One saint was asked by a reporter from the West, "Are you God?" The saint responded without hesitation, "Yes, I am," to which everyone in attendance seemed stunned. Then after a brief pause, he continued, "And so are you. The only difference between you and me," he said, "is that I know it and you doubt it."

You are a piece of God. You are a Divine creation—a being of light who showed up here as a human being at the exact moment you were supposed to. Your body will depart at precisely the right moment as well. But you're not that body you behold, nor are you its personality or any of its possessions and accomplishments. You are the beloved. A miracle. A part of the eternal perfection. A piece of the Divine intelligence that supports everything and everyone on this planet. In a world in which this Divine intelligence creates everything, there can be no accidents. Every time you experience fear, self-rejection, anxiety, guilt, or hate, you're denying your divinity and succumbing to the influences of that insidious ego mind that has convinced you of your disconnection to God.

Author U. S. Andersen wrote an inspiring book many years ago called *Three Magic Words*. Andersen writes about the ability to become a miracle worker and to live up to the ideal of the promise made by Jesus Christ: "Even the least among you can do all that I have done, and even greater things." The author doesn't reveal what the three magic words are until the end of the book, when the reader discovers that the words are "You are God." Not God in the sense of "above all others and better than everyone else," but in the sense of being eternally connected to your Source, the ever-present power of love that never abandons you and never runs dry. You can rely on this Source if you remind yourself that it includes you at all times.

DAY 19

Trust the
Spiritual Source

We need to continually trust that the organizing intelligence of our Source, which is always operating in the universe, is ever-mindful, and provides us with every blessing in abundance. But how do we trust a Source that we can't see or touch? That is our subject for today.

Imagine a camera that can accomplish photographic feats that no camera has performed prior to this time. For instance, it can take pictures through concrete walls, or in the dark without benefit of a flash. But most ingeniously, it can record a person's thoughts, producing an exact pictorial likeness of what any subject is imagining at the moment the shutter snaps. And inside the camera's package is an invitation to talk with the creator of this remarkable device. The printed material states that he'll be happy to discuss how and why his invention works, along with the amazing results that it can produce.

The conversation you'd have with the creator of your new miracle gadget probably wouldn't begin with the things you thought he'd forgotten or should or shouldn't have done. And it's unlikely that you'd complain about the price or how it was marketed, or attempt to convince him that you had more expertise. Instead, you'd probably use the opportunity to maximize your ability to work with your new camera and derive the greatest pleasure possible as it performed the tasks it was designed to accomplish.

It's safe to say that you'd approach the creator of something you can see, touch, and use—but haven't a clue as to how it came into being—with deference, respect, and awe because you'd be so eager to absorb all that he has to offer. If this analogy is unclear, you might want to quit reading at this point and seek an expert to remove your blinders!

When you finally "get" that your Source is all-knowing, you can approach the act of spiritual communication from an entirely ego-less perspective. Your discourse must begin with a recognition that it's impossible for you to be ignored. You can link up to all-knowingness by thinking like God—that is, by being an energetic match in your thoughts and actions, by being grateful, and by thinking of others and offering them what you desire.

Since you know that when you ask, it is given, you must next ask God for what you want. I'm not implying that you should beg, or think that you've been overlooked, but rather ask in a way that takes the form of a vibrational shift in energy. So you'd request to be an instrument of God's abundance, for instance, instead of pleading for cash. You'd simply match what you want with the All-Encompassing Abundance that is your Spiritual Source.

Note that anything and everything keeping you from appreciating your Spiritual Source is an impediment. This particularly includes relying on someone else or some organization without examining the truths that they insist you believe. While this may come as a surprise, Jesus wasn't a Christian, Buddha wasn't a Buddhist, and Mohammed wasn't a Muslim. These were Divine spiritual beings who came here as emissaries of truth... yet when their truths were organized, there were the horrors of inquisitions, mass murders, crusades, and holy wars all in the name of "God."

Those who claim to represent these Divine beings of truth frequently do so from a decidedly non-spiritual perspective. When an organization includes some, yet excludes others, they're announcing that they're not actually preaching or teaching truth. Since God excludes no one, any religious organization that does isn't affiliated with Him. God is all-knowing. No one else is, unless they experience pure God-realization... and those beings who have ever lived among us belong to a very small club.

No one else can intervene for you in your efforts to commune with your Source of Being: You shouldn't rely on organizations, gurus, rituals, temples, or any other outside sources as the means to make conscious contact with God. Instead, you must approach the All-Knowing Source in silent communion, and be willing to listen and receive guidance. You must speak in words of your own choosing with statements that tell God: "I know that You are all-knowing and could never forget me. I desire to align with Your all-knowingness, to have the faith that I can attract into my life all the goodness, peace, and abundance that You are. I will stay in this place of trust, for I am here to serve. I am grateful for all that You are, and all that You allow me to be."

Co-creating with Spirit

Keep in mind that you can't co-create with anyone, including your Spiritual Source, unless you're in a place of trust and harmony. To that end, you must suspend your false self (ego) and stop all thoughts of resistance before you can participate in creating the inspired life you desire, in perfect symmetry with Spirit. Whatever you ask of your Source in your prayerful communion will no longer be a wish or a hope—it will become a reality in your mind, just as it is in the mind of God. The how and when of its arrival, which have always troubled the ego, are no longer issues.

You maintain your optimism with thoughts such as *I desire it, it's in harmony with my Source,* or *It's on its way—there's nothing to fuss about.* And then you can relax and surrender to your knowing. As Ernest Holmes reminds us: "The thing we surrender to becomes our power." I know that the term *surrender* is generally associated with defeat, but there's no victor or victim when surrendering to God—this isn't about winning or losing.

You see, what you're doing here is giving up your false self in favor of returning to your authentic one. And when you do, you'll meet your spiritual creator and become empowered to live in the same vibration with It. You'll become co-creators by surrendering and joining the all-knowing, all-creating Force that allows everything to come into existence. Then your knowing replaces your doubts, and "Divine will prevails at all times." Only now, *you* are in harmony with that Divine will.

DAY 20

Wisdom Is Avoiding All Thoughts That Weaken You

Every single thought we have can be assessed in terms of whether it strengthens or weakens us. Today we are focusing on how to avoid thoughts that weaken us.

In fact, there's a simple muscle test you can do to try out any thought that you're having in the present moment. It works like this: Hold your arm out to your side, and have someone else attempt to push your arm down while you resist.

Think of telling a lie, and notice how much weaker you are than if you think of a truth. This can be done for any thought that elicits an emotional reaction.

In his book titled *Power vs. Force*, David R. Hawkins, M.D., elaborates on this method and provides a map of consciousness to show you how every thought computes to either weaken or strengthen you. Authentic wisdom is the ability to monitor yourself at all times to determine your relative state of weakness or strength, and to shift out of those thoughts that weaken you. In this way, you keep yourself in an upbeat, higher state of consciousness, and you prevent your thoughts from weakening every single organ of your body. When you use your mind to empower you, you're appealing to that which uplifts and raises your spirits.

Power urges you to live and perform at your own highest level, and it is compassionate. Force, on the other hand, involves movement. This is unlike power, which is a standing field that never moves against anything. Because force is in motion, it always creates a counterforce. That counterforce constantly consumes, and must be fed, energy. Rather than being compassionate, force is associated with judgment, competition, and controlling others. For example, in an athletic event, your thoughts are on overpowering your opponent, being better than another, and playing and winning at any cost. The entire muscular structure of your body is actually weakened, because thoughts of force weaken you.

On the other hand, if in the midst of an athletic event you can keep your thoughts on performing at your highest capacity, on using your inner strength to muster the energy to be as efficient as it's possible for you to be, and to have great respect for your God-given abilities, you will actually be empowering yourself. A thought of force requires a counterforce, and a battle that weakens; while a thought of power strengthens you, since no counterforce is called into play to consume your energy. Power thoughts energize you, since they make no demands on you.

Thoughts That Weaken You

If a simple thought will make the muscles of your arm go weak or strong, imagine what it must be doing to all of the other muscles and organs of your body! Your heart is a muscle that's weakened by thoughts that disempower you. Your kidneys, liver, lungs, and intestines are all surrounded by muscles that are affected by your thoughts.

The thought that makes most people the weakest is shame, which produces humiliation. The importance of forgiving yourself cannot be stated strongly enough. If you carry around thoughts of shame about what you've done in the past, you're weakening yourself both physically and emotionally. Similarly, if you use a technique of shame and humiliation on anyone to get *them* to reform, you're going to create a weakened person who will never become empowered until those shameful and humiliating thoughts are removed. Removing your own thoughts of shame involves a willingness to let go, to see your past behaviors as lessons you had to learn, and to reconnect to your Source through prayer and meditation.

After shame, guilt and apathy thoughts make you the weakest. They produce the emotions of blame and despair. To live in guilt is to use up your present moments being immobilized over what has already transpired. No amount of guilt will ever undo what's been done. If your past behavior mobilizes you to learn from your mistakes, this is not guilt; it's learning from the past. But to wallow in the present moment over your so-called errors is guilt, and it can only take place now.

Releasing guilt is like removing a huge weight from your shoulders. Guilt is released through the empowering thought of love and respect for yourself. You empower yourself with love and respect, letting go of standards of perfection and refusing to use up the precious currency of your life, the now, with thoughts that only continue to frustrate and weaken you. Instead, you can vow to be better than you used to be, which is the true test of nobility.

Apathetic thoughts create despair. They are the thoughts that keep you from being engaged in life. Apathy stems from self-pity and a need to be entertained continually to avoid boredom. You can never be apathetic or lonely if you love the person you're alone with. Every moment of every day presents an unlimited number of options for living fully and being connected to life. You don't need a television or a radio constantly blaring to avoid apathy. You have your own mind, which is a kingdom of limitless potential.

You have the choice each day to wake up and say, "Good morning, God" or "Good God, morning!" It's always a choice. Any moments that you fill with thoughts of boredom and apathy will truly weaken you physically, emotionally, and spiritually. To me, it's an insult to this wondrous universe filled with a hundred million miracles to ever allow myself to think thoughts of boredom or apathy.

The other prominent thoughts that compete to make you weak include fear and anger. Both of these categories of thought employ force, which produces a counterforce and an inner atmosphere of tension and weakness. When you're afraid, you've moved away from love. Remember, "Perfect love casteth out all fear." What you fear, you resent and ultimately begin to hate. Thus, the dichotomy of hate and fear is at work within you, always weakening you.

Every thought you have in which you're in a state of fear keeps you away from your purpose, and is simultaneously weakening you. Your fearful thoughts are inviting you to stay immobilized. When you find yourself in a fearful mode, stop right there and invite God onto the scene. Turn fear over to your Senior Partner with these words: "I don't know how to deal with this, but I know I'm connected to You, the miraculous creative force in this universe. I'll move my ego out of the way and turn it over to You." Try it. You'll be surprised by how quickly that higher energy of love will nullify and dissolve your fearful thoughts and empower you at the same time.

Anger, likewise, is an emotional reaction to thoughts that say, "I want the world to be the way I want it, not the way it is; therefore, I'm angry." Anger is often justified as normal, but it will always make you weak; and as this principle reminds you, wisdom is avoiding all thoughts that weaken you. You don't have to be angry to right a wrong or work toward a better world. When you become more peaceful, you will only have peace to give away. Moments of frustration won't trigger anger; they'll help you be more aware, and then they'll spur you on to a solution.

Every thought of anger moves you away from love and into violence and vengeance, which are forces that spur counterforces, weakening everyone involved. All of these thoughts of shame, guilt, apathy, fear, and anger are energies, since everything in our universe is a vibrating frequency. Those that weaken you are low/slow frequencies, and they can only be dissolved by bringing the higher/faster energies of Spirit to their presence.

DAY 21

Thoughts That Strengthen You

Your thoughts come with an accompanying energy, so you might as well shift to those that empower you. When you move from a thought that's a very low-energy vibration to one of a higher frequency, you go from weak to strong. When your thoughts are on blaming others, you're weakened. But when you shift to loving and trusting others, you become strong. Today we are going to investigate the thoughts that make us stronger.

Once you realize that what you think about is the source of your experience of reality, then you'll begin to pay more attention to what you're thinking in any given moment.

Many years ago, in a tremendously popular audio program called *The Strangest Secret*, Earl Nightingale taught many of us that we become what we think about all day long. Your thoughts determine whether you're being empowered or weakened—whether you're happy or sad, successful or not. Everything is a thought that you carry around with you. Happy thoughts create happy molecules. Your health is determined largely by the thoughts you have. Passionately think that you won't get a cold, and your body will react to your thoughts. Refuse to entertain thoughts of fatigue, jet lag, or headaches, and your body responds to your thoughts.

Your mind tells your body to produce the chemicals it needs to keep you healthy. Give someone a sugar pill and convince them that it's an anti-arthritic drug, and that person's body will react to the placebo with the increased production of anti-arthritic energies. The mind is a powerful tool in creating health. It also creates divine relationships, abundance, harmony in business—and even parking places! If your thoughts are focused on what you want to attract in your life, and you maintain that thought with the passion of an absolute intention, you'll eventually act upon that intention, because the ancestor to every single action is a thought.

The greater your desire, the more thought horsepower you'll apply to its fulfillment. The more intense your desirous thoughts, the greater the measure of love going into your asking and your labor will be—and coming in contact with love is the very essence of Spirit and inspiration. Weak thoughts will attract doubt and weakness, which will cause you to experience monotony and drudgery in your efforts. With monotony, you'll give up, but with love, you'll be available to abundant hope.

For example, I find it impossible to think in boring terms when it comes to my writing. My thoughts are so intense that I feel love for what I'm doing and joyful when I even pass by my writing space. I get a warm feeling throughout my body because my desire to convey these ideas and express what

I'm learning each day is so intense that it matches up with the spiritual energy of the Source of All Creation. Obviously when I'm asking for guidance, my thoughts or queries go out to my Spirit, which then matches up with the Divine Source.

I know that my thoughts are energy and that those harmonizing with Spirit will align to activate the creation process. I love watching all this flow so perfectly and being in harmony with the Force that's responsible for all of creation. I know deep within me that I can participate in the activation of this Force to bring into reality the manifestation of my spiritually aligned desires.

If you make this an inner mantra: *I intend to feel good*, you can think of and picture yourself experiencing joy regardless of what's going on around you. You can remind yourself that whatever you desire is on its way, in amounts greater than ever imagined. If you keep this thought uppermost in mind, then before long, the All-Creating Source will conspire to bring your thought into your physical life. Most important, you'll begin to act on your thought and receive Divine guidance.

The most empowering thoughts you can have are those of peace, joy, love, acceptance, and willingness. These thoughts don't create a counterforce. Powerful, joyful, loving thoughts stem from your willingness to allow the world to be as it is. Then you're in a state of inner bliss where serenity replaces fighting, reverence for all of life substitutes for craving and anxiety, and understanding supplants scorn. You become an optimist. Rather than seeing the glass as half empty, it's always half full.

All of this is nothing more than a conscious decision on your part to be in charge of your thinking. Be aware at any given moment in your life that you always have a choice about the thoughts you allow in your mind. No one else can put a thought there. Regardless of the circumstances you find yourself in, *it is your choice*. Choose to replace disempowering, weakening thoughts with thoughts of a higher spiritual frequency.

Don't convince yourself that it can't be done or it's easier said than done. Your mind is yours to control. You are the creator and selector of your thoughts. You can change them at will. It is your God-given inheritance, your corner of freedom that no one can take away. No one can have control of your thoughts without your consent. So choose to avoid thoughts that weaken you, and you will know true wisdom. *It is your choice!*

Afterword

Experience has taught me that the laws of the material world truly do not apply in the presence of God-realization. And I know that I have the choice to live at this level of awareness and be successful and find inner peace. When I do so, it seems that the world changes: Animals behave differently than their biological genetics would seem to allow, people at a distance seem to hear me telepathically and respond to my highest thoughts, objects seem to materialize in defiance of what scientists say is possible, and healing takes place in spite of modern medicine saying otherwise. In other words, miracles seem to be ordinary.

The world looks like a place where everything is possible, where restrictions and limitations are non-existent, and where the power of our Creator seems to roll right up and land at my feet, begging me to hop on board and witness the infinite possibilities it offers. This is how I feel when I align myself to Spirit: Pleased with myself inside because I know something that so few ever come to realize, but humble and awestruck on the outside at the miraculousness of it all!

I've come to understand that when one thing appears to be going wrong, I can see clearly that 10 things are going right. For example, if my cell phone isn't working, I can note that my health is fine, my family is safe, the ocean is calm for swimming, my bank account has a surplus, my electricity is fully functional, and on and on it goes. I automatically shift my attention away from what's going wrong and onto what's right—this then becomes my point of attraction and I attract more of what I'm focused on, whereas at an earlier time in my life, I'd attract more of what was going wrong because that was my point of attraction.

How sublimely beautiful the world now looks to me from this magnificent place! No longer do I stay focused on and attract more of what's going wrong, for I've learned to place my attention on what's right, what's working, and what's aligned with the All-Creating Spirit.

Rather than hoping, wishing, and even praying for an outcome, my inner world aligns with the idea that what I desire is feasible and on its way. This kind of inspired knowing frees me from anxiety and worry. I affirm: *It's on its way; there's absolutely nothing to fuss about.* And I leave the time of its arrival into my life in the hands of the All-Knowing, Always-Creative Spiritual Source. I find that I no longer question the Creator of the Universe because I'm at peace with the timing of everything. I know enough now not to push the river, not to demand that the timetable of my ego be the same as God's.

What I so sincerely want to share here is that the feeling of being completely in harmony with our Source generates not only success and inner peace, but miracles everywhere. I have the delicious spine-tingling sensation of bliss as I observe and interact in this world from the wondrous vista of being inspired. These words from *A Course in Miracles* ring true for me: "All that must be recognized, however, is that birth was not the beginning, and death is not the end." This is the knowing that I have from this infinite spiritual perspective.

It's my intention to continue to live what my mind knows, rather than only what my eyes see. And my mind knows that we're all in a universe that has a creative, organizing intelligence supporting it. I know that it flows through me, and God willing, I'll assist you to live the life that you came here to live. There can be no greater blessing!

I send you love, I surround you with light, and I invite you to enjoy success and inner peace as you live your life aligned with Spirit.

About the Author

Affectionately called the "father of motivation" by his fans, **Dr. Wayne W. Dyer** was an internationally renowned author, speaker, and pioneer in the field of self-development. Over the four decades of his career he wrote more than 40 books, including *Manifest Your Destiny*, *Wisdom of the Ages*, *There's a Spiritual Solution to Every Problem*, and the *New York Times* best-sellers *10 Secrets for Success and Inner Peace*, *The Power of Intention*, *Inspiration*, *Change Your Thoughts – Change Your Life*, *Excuses Begone!*, *Wishes Fulfilled*, and *I Can See Clearly Now*. He also created numerous audio programs and videos, and appeared on thousands of radio and television shows, including *The Today Show*, *The Tonight Show*, and *Oprah*.

Wayne held a doctorate in educational counselling from Wayne State University, was an associate professor at St. John's University in New York, and honored a lifetime commitment to education and finding the Higher Self. In 2015 he left his body, returning to Infinite Source to embark on his next adventure.

www.drwaynedyer.com

Also by Dr. Wayne W. Dyer

BOOKS

Being in Balance

Change Your Thoughts—
Change Your Life

Don't Die with Your Music Still
in You (with Serena J. Dyer)

Everyday Wisdom

Everyday Wisdom for Success

Excuses Begone!

Getting in the Gap

Good-bye, Bumps! (children's
book with Saje Dyer)

Happiness Is the Way

I Am (children's book
with Kristina Tracy)

I Can See Clearly Now

Incredible You! (children's
book with Kristina Tracy)

The Invisible Force

It's Not What You've Got! (children's
book with Kristina Tracy)

Living an Inspired Life

Living the Wisdom of the Tao

Memories of Heaven

My Greatest Teacher
(with Lynn Lauber)

No Excuses! (children's book
with Kristina Tracy)

The Power of Awakening

The Power of Intention

The Power of Intention (gift edition)

A Promise Is a Promise

The Shift

Staying on the Path

10 Secrets for Success and Inner
Peace

Unstoppable Me! (children's
book with Kristina Tracy)

You Are What You Think

Your Ultimate Calling

Wishes Fulfilled

AUDIO PROGRAMS

Advancing Your Spirit
(with Marianne Williamson)

Applying the 10 Secrets for Success
and Inner Peace

The Caroline Myss & Wayne Dyer
Seminar

Change Your Thoughts—Change
Your Life (unabridged audiobook)

Change Your Thoughts Meditation

Divine Love

Dr. Wayne W. Dyer Unplugged
(interviews with Lisa Garr)

Everyday Wisdom (audiobook)

Excuses Begone! (available as an
audiobook and a lecture)

How to Get What You Really,
Really, Really, Really Want

I AM Wishes Fulfilled Meditation
(with James Twyman)

I Can See Clearly Now
(unabridged audiobook)

The Importance of Being
Extraordinary (with Eckhart Tolle)

Inspiration (abridged 4-CD set)

Inspirational Thoughts

Making the Shift (6-CD set)

Making Your Thoughts Work for You (with Byron Katie)

Meditations for Manifesting

101 Ways to Transform Your Life (audiobook)

The Power of Intention (abridged 4-CD set)

A Promise Is a Promise (audiobook)

Secrets of Manifesting

The Secrets of the Power of Intention (6-CD set)

10 Secrets for Success and Inner Peace

There Is a Spiritual Solution to Every Problem

The Wayne Dyer Audio Collection/CD Collection

Wishes Fulfilled (unabridged audiobook)

DVDs

Change Your Thoughts— Change Your Life

Excuses Begone!

Experiencing the Miraculous

I Can See Clearly Now

The Importance of Being Extraordinary (with Eckhart Tolle)

Inspiration

Modern Wisdom from the Ancient World

My Greatest Teacher (a film with bonus material featuring Wayne Dyer)

The Power of Intention

The Shift, the movie (available as a 1-DVD program and an expanded 2-DVD set)

10 Secrets for Success and Inner Peace

There's a Spiritual Solution to Every Problem

Wishes Fulfilled

MISCELLANEOUS

Daily Inspiration from Dr. Wayne W. Dyer Calendar (for each individual year)

The Essential Wayne Dyer Collection (comprising The Power of Intention, Inspiration, and Excuses Begone! in a single volume)

The Shift Box Set (includes The Shift DVD and The Shift tradepaper book)

All of the above are available at your local bookstore, or may be ordered by visiting:

Hay House UK: www.hayhouse.co.uk
Hay House USA: www.hayhouse.com
Hay House Australia: www.hayhouse.com.au
Hay House India: www.hayhouse.co.in

We hope you enjoyed this Hay House book. If you'd like to receive our online catalog featuring additional information on Hay House books and products, or if you'd like to find out more about the Hay Foundation, please contact:

Hay House, Inc., P.O. Box 5100, Carlsbad, CA 92018-5100
(760) 431-7695 or (800) 654-5126
(760) 431-6948 (fax) or (800) 650-5115 (fax)
www.hayhouse.com® • www.hayfoundation.org

———

Published in Australia by: Hay House Australia Pty. Ltd.,
18/36 Ralph St., Alexandria NSW 2015
Phone: 612-9669-4299 • *Fax:* 612-9669-4144
www.hayhouse.com.au

Published in the United Kingdom by: Hay House UK, Ltd.,
The Sixth Floor, Watson House, 54 Baker Street, London W1U 7BU
Phone: +44 (0)20 3927 7290 • *Fax:* +44 (0)20 3927 7291
www.hayhouse.co.uk

Published in India by: Hay House Publishers India,
Muskaan Complex, Plot No. 3, B-2, Vasant Kunj, New Delhi 110 070
Phone: 91-11-4176-1620 • *Fax:* 91-11-4176-1630
www.hayhouse.co.in

———

Access New Knowledge.
Anytime. Anywhere.

Learn and evolve at your own pace
with the world's leading experts.

www.hayhouseU.com

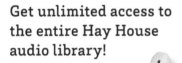

CONNECT WITH
HAY HOUSE
ONLINE

🌐 hayhouse.co.uk   f @hayhouse

📷 @hayhouseuk   🐦 @hayhouseuk

▶ @hayhouseuk   ♪ @hayhouseuk

Find out all about our latest books & card decks • Be the first to know about exclusive discounts • Interact with our authors in live broadcasts • Celebrate the cycle of the seasons with us • Watch free videos from your favourite authors • Connect with like-minded souls

'The gateways to wisdom and knowledge are always open.'

Louise Hay